The Logic of Questions and Answers

The Logic of Questions and Answers

NUEL D. BELNAP, JR.

THOMAS B. STEEL, JR.

Bibliography of the Theory of Questions and Answers
by Urs Egli and Hubert Schleichert

New Haven and London, Yale University Press

1976

Designed by John O. C. McCrillis
and set in IBM Selectric Press Roman type.
Printed in the United States of America by
The Alpine Press, Inc.,
South Braintree, Massachusetts.

Published in Great Britain, Europe, Africa, and
Asia (except Japan) by
Yale University Press, Ltd., London.
Distributed in Latin America by Kaiman & Polon,
Inc., New York City; in Australia and New
Zealand by Book & Film Services, Artarmon, N.S.W.,
Australia; in Japan by John Weatherhill, Inc., Tokyo

Library of Congress Cataloging in Publication Data
Belnap, Nuel D   1930–
    The logic of questions and answers.

    Bibliography: p.
    Includes index.
    1. Question (Logic)   2. Question-answering sys-
tems.   3. Formal languages.   I. Steel, Thomas B.,
1929–   joint author.   II. Title.
BC199.Q4B44   160   75–27761
ISBN 0-300-01962-9

Contents

The Logic of Questions and Answers

Introduction

What is the logic of questions and answers? The name erotetic logic was coined by Prior and Prior in 1955 to refer to the logic of questions, and evidently should be thought of in analogy to the logic of statements. But getting the analogy right is, of course, crucial. Absolutely the wrong thing is to think it is a logic in the sense of a deductive system, since one would thus be driven to the pointless task of inventing an inferential scheme in which questions, or interrogatives, could serve as premises and conclusions. This is to say that what one wants erotetic logic to imitate of the rest of logic is not its proof theory but rather its other two grand parts, grammar (syntax) and semantics.

The right thing is to imagine questioner and respondent in possession of a common language presumably sufficient for purposes of scientific communication, and then ask how this language could be enriched so that it could be used to ask and answer questions in an orderly, fruitful way. This suggests a twofold task. On the object-language level we want to create a carefully designed apparatus permitting the asking and answering of questions. On the meta-language level we want to elaborate a set of concepts useful for categorizing, evaluating, and relating questions and answers. In order to limit our scope, we shall not deal directly with questions as they

This paper, except for the introduction and chapter 4, was largely completed in 1968 and has been but little revised since then. Chapters 1–3 were written for the most part by N.D.B., while the introduction and chapter 4 are primarily the work of T.B.S., though we both assume responsibility for the whole. We are grateful to the System Development Corporation for substantial support of the research reported herein and to the National Science Foundation (Grant: GS 28478) for partial support.

occur in ordinary English. Instead, we shall at all times suppose both the assertional language and the erotetic language to be formal. Nevertheless, we shall give a number of examples indicating how questions in English would be translated into questions in our formal language. We hope thus to illuminate the question-answer situation in English in much the same way that formal logic illuminates the inference situation in English, in order to thereby contribute to our understanding of the erotetic "deep structure" of natural language. Although we have a certain interest in explicating questions and answers in English, our primary aim here is rather to design a good formal notation for questions and answers and a good set of concepts for talking about them.

Over and above the obvious intellectual motivation for this investigation, we have also been stimulated and to some extent guided by the potential applicability of erotetic logic to current problems in data processing technology. We have thus included in the last chapter a brief discussion of the relationship between the formal theory and its possible applications.

There is one conceptual feature of the development below that is so in contrast to those analyses of questions typical of most previous data processing specialists that it deserves special mention. The meaning of a question addressed to a query system is not to be identified with how the system processes the query (and is not to be identified with a program at any level), but rather it is to be identified with the range of answers that the question permits. That is, for a query system and a user to agree on the meaning of a question is for there to be agreement as to what counts as an answer to the question, regardless of how, or if, any answer is produced. This conceptual feature is important because

only if one has an analysis of questions that is independent
of computers and programs can he sensibly ask such questions
as these: What sorts of questions would I really like to ask?
For various sorts of questions, is my query system able to
answer them? (Is it "complete" in these respects?) For various
sorts of questions, is my query system efficient, inefficient,
improvable, etc.? And, in general, given a sort of question
specified in computer-independent terms, how should it
relate to my own particular query system?

Before beginning the body of the text, we wish to provide
the reader with a summary of it as something of a road map.
While our examples will often, and in this summary exclusively, be drawn from ordinary English, it is fundamental to
this enterprise that there be an underlying assertoric apparatus. The details of the erotetic program are dependent on
the nature of this assertoric underpinning. We envision an
applied first-order functional calculus with identity, having
provision for both predicate and function constants, supple-
mented by a provision for making category distinctions.

The notion of a *direct answer* to a question is basic. A
direct answer is a piece of language that completely, but just
completely, answers the question. A direct answer may be
true or false. What is crucial is that it be effectively decidable
whether a given piece of language is a direct answer to a
specific question.

A *question* is an abstract thing, and the notation for it is
an *interrogative*. The interrogative is said to *put* the question.
An *elementary* question has two parts, a *subject* and a *request*. The subject presents a set of alternatives, and the request identifies how many of the true alternatives are desired
in the answer and what sort of claims for completeness and

distinctness are to be made. The set of direct answers can be determined from the possible combinations of alternatives composed consistently with the terms of the request.

Questions whose subjects present an explicit, finite list of alternatives are called *whether-questions.* Thus, *Is John going home?* presents the alternatives: *John is going home,* and *John is not going home,* and these two assertions are the direct answers to the question. Questions whose subject presents a set of alternatives, possibly infinite, by reference to a matrix and possibly a category condition are called *which-questions.* Thus, *Which positive integer is the smallest odd prime?* presents an infinity of alternatives by reference to the matrix *x is the smallest odd prime* and the category condition *x is an integer.* Substitution of a numeral for "*x*" in the matrix generates an alternative. We note here that a distinction between real and nominal alternatives may be necessary in instances where the category is sufficiently large that we cannot have names for all the entities, e.g., the category of real numbers.

We parse the request into three components. The first, *selection-size-specification,* is a quantifier-like indication of the number of true alternatives requested, e.g., at least one, all, 5%, etc. The second component of the request is a *completeness-claim-specification,* which indicates whether the questioner wishes the answer to include a claim concerning the degree to which the selection-size-specification is met. Finally, the *distinctness-claim-specification* is that component of the request that asks for an answer to address the issue of whether the alternatives are really distinct as opposed to being nominally distinct, namely, "7" as opposed to "VII." It is not the case that all types of questions require all components of the request.

Direct answers, then, consist of a conjunction of selected alternatives, the magnitude of the selection being determined by the selection-size-specification, and, when appropriate, claims regarding completeness and distinctness.

Whether and which questions are *elementary questions.* Other sorts of questions are amenable to analysis, including compounds of elementary questions, hypothetical questions, conditional questions, and the like. These are discussed in varying degrees below.

Finally, some observations on erotetic semantics are in order. We arrive at the conclusion that the most useful formulation of the concept of *presuppositions* of a question is:

> A question, Q, presupposes a statement, A, if and only if, the truth of A is a logically necessary condition for there being some true answer to Q.

Rigorous analyses subject to this definition allow resolution of such linguistically troublesome questions as: *Have you stopped beating your wife?*

We treat interrogatives as *true* or *false* according to whether they do or do not have any true answers. It then makes sense to apply other semantical notions such as logical truth, consistency, implication and equivalence to interrogatives in a more or less standard way.

This brief summary is like a view of the earth from an orbiting satellite: only the main features of the terrain are apparent, and even many of these are obscured by clouds. It is now appropriate to turn to the ground and examine the details.

1   The Grammar of Elementary Questions

This chapter elaborates in some detail the grammar of elementary questions and culminates in 1.34 with the definition of the paramount grammatical relation, the question-answer relationship itself. But because we want our grammar to be *good* grammar, we must give detailed consideration to its design; so there is much to come first.

1.0   The Assertoric Underpinnings   In spite of the fact that our examples will be drawn from natural language and our introductory exposition comprehensible in these terms alone, it remains true that the course of our analysis is heavily influenced by the particular formal assertoric* language to which our erotetic apparatus is to be added. Things appropriate here would not be appropriate were the underlying assertoric apparatus differently conceived. For this reason, and although most of the remainder of section 1.0 may be skipped without profound loss, we begin with a brief description of a formal language L, for which we want to devise a logic of questions. Inasmuch as we have no intention of using L in this study, we shall not exhibit any part of it but merely describe it. And although we speak as of a unique language L, we really have in mind any language from a large family satisfying certain

---

*There is no good name for the sort of logic other logicians do. We will use the expression "assertoric logic" from time to time, but logic has to do with propositions or sentences both considered as well as asserted. "Declarative logic" has the same effect and also seems to commit one to a grammatical point of view. (It was to avoid this latter commitment that we prefer "erotetic logic" over "interrogative logic.") The most accurate names would be "sentential logic" or "propositional logic," but, alas, these terms are already used for the logic of connectives.

conditions. For those familiar with standard formal systems, we may describe L as a straightforward applied first-order functional calculus with identity (Church 1956, p. 281), having provision for both predicate and function constants. But, we add generalized conjunctions and disjunctions, and also somewhat nonstandard provisions for making "type" or "category" distinctions, as in a many-sorted logic.

L is supplied with a countable list of *individual constants* and a denumerable list of *individual variables.* We use *w, x, y,* and *z,* sometimes with subscripts, as metalinguistic variables ranging over the individual variables of L. L has also a list of *n-ary function constants* and a list of *n-ary predicate constants.* We use *f* and *g* as metalinguistic variables ranging over the former, and *F* and *G* as ranging over the latter, their degree being left to context. L has signs = of identity, & of conjunction, V of disjunction, $^{-}$ (or sometimes $\sim$) of negation, $\supset$ of material "implication," and $\equiv$ of material "equivalence." L, further, has the signs $\exists$ and $\forall$, used in forming the existential quantifier, $\exists x$ and universal quantifier $\forall x$ respectively. Parentheses are used in the usual way, and *terms* and *formulas* are defined recursively as usual, with the following exception: we shall suppose that if $A_1, \ldots, A_n$ are each formulas, then so also is not only $(A_1 \& A_2)$ but also $(A_1 \& \ldots \& A_n)$. Similarly, $(A_1 V \ldots V A_n)$ will be taken as a formula. These generalized conjunctions and disjunctions do not increase our powers of assertoric expression, since we wish to interpret $(A_1 \& \ldots \& A_n)$ as logically equivalent to $(((\ldots (A_1 \& A_2) \ldots) \& A_{n-1}) \& A_n)$, and similarly for V, but the availability of the generalized forms, while strictly inessential, makes some of our erotetic machinery run more smoothly.

a, b, and *c,* sometimes with subscripts, range over terms while *A, B,* and occasionally other capitals so declared, sometimes with subscripts, range over formulas. Terms without free variables are called *names.* Formulas without free variables are *statements,* and formulas with exactly n free variables are *n-place conditions.* $Ax_1 \ldots x_n$ is an arbitrary formula, the use of this notation being subject to the following convention: given $Ax_1 \ldots x_n$, $Ab_1 \ldots b_n$ is defined as the result of replacing each free occurrence of each variable x_i in $Ax_1 \ldots x_n$ by an occurrence of b_i, taking the usual precautions to prevent variables turning up bound in $Ab_1 \ldots b_n$, where they ought to be free. (Henceforth we will assume without mention that such precautions are taken.)

   In order to allow the making of appropriate category distinctions, we also suppose that some of the one-place conditions of L are set aside in an effectively specified list of *elementary category conditions,* and we shall suppose that for each name a, the condition $x = a$ is among the elementary category conditions. The whole set of *category conditons* is specified recursively as follows: all elementary category conditions are category conditions, and if Ax and Bx are category conditions containing exactly the same variable free, then $(Ax$ & $Bx)$ and $(Ax \lor Bx)$ are category conditions, as well as any result of changing variables (either free or bound) in Ax. In order to implement the category apparatus, we suppose that for each category condition there is defined a set of associated names as follows. For each elementary category condition Ax, there is defined, as part of the grammar of the language L, an effectively specified (recursive, decidable) set of names called *the nominal category determined by Ax*: it must be $\{a\}$ if Ax is $x = a$. It is assumed that if Ax and By differ only in their (free or bound) variables, then they determine the same nominal category. If Ax is a nonelementary category condition, then if it has the form $(Bx$ & $Cx)$ or $(Bx \lor Cx)$, the nominal category determined by Ax is defined respectively as the intersection or union of those determined by Bx and Cx.

Allowing the set of category conditions to be closed under changes of variable, conjunction, and disjunction gives us a certain flexibility and costs us nothing. On the other hand, were we to have insisted that the set of category conditions be closed under negation, restrictive consequences would have arisen, as we point out below.

This completes the grammar of L. Turning now to its semantics, we define a *candidate interpretation* as an ordered couple consisting of a nonempty domain of individuals, D, together with an *interpretation function* taking the various variables and constants as arguments. This function yields as values individuals in D (for individual variables and constants), functions on D (for function constants), and relations on D (for predicate constants).

Then, when a is a term, A a formula, M a candidate interpretation, and i an individual in the domain of M, we shall suppose "*a denotes i in M*" and "*A is true (false) in M*" to be defined in the usual way. By the *range of M* of a one-place condition Ax, we mean the set of individuals i in the domain of M such that Ax is true in that interpretation M' which is like M except in assigning i to the free variable x of Ax. The range in M of a category condition is also called the *real category* determined by that condition in M, or sometimes the *real range* of the category condition.

Because category conditions differing only in their free or bound variables determine the same nominal and real categories, there is no erotetically relevant difference between them. We therefore say that such conditions are *equivalent*, and we write Cx for the set of conditions equivalent to Cx.

The semantic implementation of the category apparatus is accomplished by means of our definition of "interpretation": an *interpretation* is defined as a candidate interpretation M, in which, for every category condition Ax, every name in the *nominal* category determined by Ax denotes in M some individual in the *real* category determined by Ax in M. Our definitions are such that if elementary category conditions have this property, then all category conditions will, which is why closing category conditions under conjunction and disjunction was without cost. And it is to preserve this feature that we do not close them under negation.

We suppose the usual semantic notions of *consistency, validity* or *logical truth, logical implication,* and *logical equivalence* to be defined in the usual ways with the help of the notion of interpretation. For example, A logically implies B if there is no interpretation in which A is true and B false. These classical notions are not without fault, as one of us is elsewhere on record as arguing (Anderson and Belnap 1975), and they lead to certain anomalies in the erotetic field itself. Nevertheless, they are the simplest concepts for our purposes, and in penetrating new territory, it seems best to take along familiar tools. See section 3.1 for the definitions.

Whenever we speak of truth, falsity, denotation, or range without explicit mention of an interpretation, we shall suppose some *principal interpretation* to which these are relative. In particular, to make our examples readable, we shall often use an expression like "*x is a boy*" as if it were part of our formal language L. And when we do so, we intend that the expression be treated as if it had the form $F(x)$, with the principal interpretation giving the ordinary meaning to the words involved.

Such is the basic grammatical and semantic machinery we

require. We do not suppose L to have any particular axioms
or rules of derivation or other proof-theoretical machinery,
the fundamental grammatical and semantic concepts outlined
above being adequate.

1.1 *Answers* Since we are designing a useful logic, we shall
want all the questions we formalize to be clear. For there is
little point in troubling with a formal system if its issue is
obscurity. In the spirit of Braithewaite's "no calculus without
calculation," we want users of this logic to be able to calcu-
late what counts as an answer to the questions we formalize.
For this reason, the scope of our formalization is confined to
the situation in which what counts as an answer to a given
question is well defined in advance.

   Expressly excluded from formalization are the problem-
solving situation and the "Please relieve my vague puzzlement" situation. The kind of questions we deal with are asked
not so much to relieve a vaguely defined mental anxiety as to
seek some definite piece of information. Omitted on these
grounds would be such deceptively simple questions as "Who
is that man living next door?" Although this looks super-
ficially like a definite information-seeking question, reflection
leads us to see that it is very hard to predict in advance just
what kind of answer would satisfy the questioner: does he
want a proper name or, perhaps, a description? And if a
description, is it one involving occupation, family connection,
previous acquaintance, or what? Our thought is that he
doesn't really know himself what he wants, but after your
reply, he will tell you if your answer relieves his anxiety and,
perhaps, ask a clearer question.

   It is well to remark at the outset our awareness that we are
leaving out some of the very most interesting kinds of ques-

tions. The class of questions asked in such a way as to give little indication of what would count as an answer includes not only many distinctively philosophical questions, such as "What is the relation between thought and language?" or "What is a number?" but also such scientific questions as "Why are there so many different kinds of subatomic particles?" or "How do children learn language?" We might also add to this list, reflexively, "What is a good account of the question-answer situation?"

Nevertheless, though we do not presume to formalize such questions, our logic is hardly "severed" from the "large class of interesting problems" they raise, as Hintikka (1974) appears to believe. Indeed, there are at least two intimate connections. First, by offering the ideal of a clear question and exploring its nature in depth, we substantially increase our understanding of how unclear questions are unclear and what it would be like for them to be clear. For example, many an investigation in the philosophy of science can be construed as a search for a way to make it quite definite what counts as an answer to questions such as these; and philosophical positions can often be classified according to what sort of thing they would take as an answer to certain kinds of questions. (Hiż 1962 discusses some of the problems raised by what-questions.) Second, our erotetic repertoire is designed to offer anyone with a vague puzzlement a rich storehouse of clear questions on which to draw so that such a person could improve the efficiency of his communication. Our aim is to not to leave natural language where it is but to better it.

Let us turn, thus, to questions for which what counts as an answer as well defined. To each such question there corresponds a set of statements which are *directly* responsive. A member of this set may, indeed, be either true or false, but in either case it is the sort of thing which tells the questioner exactly what he wants to know, neither more nor less. We follow Harrah in terming such a statement a *direct answer.* A direct answer, then, is what counts as completely, but just completely, answering the question. If we were to put the matter psychologically, we would say that a direct answer is precisely the kind of response the questioner *intends* to elicit with his question. The crucial point is that a direct answer must provide an unarguably final resolution to the question.

In order to highlight the concept of a direct answer by contrasting it with its close relatives, let us consider the sample question

(1)   *What is the freezing point of water, in degrees Fahrenheit, under standard conditions?*

We should count as direct answers to (1) both the true sentence, "*The freezing point of water under standard conditions is 32°F,*" and the false sentence, "*The freezing point of water under standard conditions is 0°F.*" On the other hand, although a direct answer need not be true, it is essential that it have the correct *form* in order to be counted as the sort of thing the question calls for: "*The freezing point of water under standard conditions is given in The Handbook of Chemistry and Physics*" is not a direct answer to (1), since it does no more than provide the questioner with a method by which he may find out for himself the true and direct answer to (1). There is another point about the "*Handbook*" response, and this is that it does not finish the task set by the question. After receiving it as a response, a questioner would still have work left to do in order to resolve his question. And the same is true, though in a lesser degree, of such sentences as "*The freezing point of water under standard conditions is 211*

degrees Fahrenheit above the freezing point of alcohol" or
"*The freezing point of water under standard conditions is
$(2^5)°F$.*" Consequently, though some of these may indeed
prove helpful to some questioners, none can count as a *direct*
answer: direct answers must finally and unequivocally finish
the job of answering the question and leave nothing further
to be done. Of course, a sentence like "*The freezing point of
water under standard conditions is 32°F., and its boiling
point is 212°F.*" does indeed completely answer (1). The
trouble here is that such a sentence goes on to give more information than is required by the question. A similar effect is
of concern to those who wish to design query-systems for
large data bases in such a way as to avoid inundating the user
with torrents of relevant but not precisely pertinent information. A. R. Anderson once mentioned in illustration of this
point that a boy in Little Rock once asked his mother to
explain why the light goes on when the switch is flipped. She
suggested he ask his engineer father, but the boy said he
didn't want to know *that* much about it.

Suppose the respondent replies to (1), not with the full
sentence "*The freezing point of water under standard conditions is 32°F.*", but merely with the noun "*32.*" Obviously,
its status as an answer, indeed, its very meaning, depends
upon the context of its utterance. So, since we are now pre-
paring the way for a formal analysis in which we shall not
want any assertoric meanings to be dependent on context, we
shall not count "*32*" as a direct answer to (1). Rather, we
shall treat it as merely an abbreviated way of saying "*The
freezing point of water under standard conditions is 32°F.,*"
and we shall call it (after Hamblin 1958) a *coded* answer.
Coded answers, including gestures and nods as well as words,
are, because of their efficiency, of enormous importance in

communication, but they must always be code for complete and unabbreviated sentences.

Because of codes, in applications of our work to linguistics the concept of *direct answerhood* should be expected to occur in the "deep structure" of the erotetic interchange, not on the surface. Lang remarks (correspondence, 1970) that "out of at least 5,000 questions and answer pairs I will be very hard pressed to find a single instance of what would qualify as a 'direct answer.' " That sounds right, but we do not see how any linguistic analysis could be even remotely adequate without having direct answerhood as a deep-structure concept.*

There is one last exclusion. It is tempting, given the question *"What's a good method of trisecting angles by means of ruler and compass?"* to count the reply *"There is no such way"* as a direct answer. It turns out, however, that discourse about questions runs more smoothly if such *corrective answers,* which challenge some presupposition of the question, are kept apart from direct answers. A cautious questioner who wishes to permit such a response as a direct answer can always ask instead, *"What's a good method of trisecting angles with ruler and compass—or isn't there any?"*

Since we have given a narrow meaning to direct answer, we need a term covering the host of more or less responsive noises that can follow upon a question. We shall use for this

*In this regard, as well, Hintikka (1974) says that we "seem to think" that "information has to be conveyed to the questioner verbally," so that a nod could not count as "a perfectly legitimate answer to a yes-or-no question." Since he gives no reference, we cannot be sure of the source of Hintikka's misunderstanding. Perhaps, though he does not cite it, it was Belnap 1969-a, which we sent him at his request in 1973. There we described our sort of question as always calling for a linguistic response, and Hintikka might have conflated "verbal" and "linguistic." We trust it goes without saying that a nod, as an answer to a yes-no question, is indeed part of the language, and that its (conventional) meaning is sentential.

purpose the word *reply*. Some replies such as the *Handbook* reply and *"That's a good question"* can only be handled in a theory of the pragmatics of questions, going in this respect beyond what we here essay. Some, however, can be usefully characterized in grammatical or semantical terms as somehow related to direct answers. For this loosely defined family we reserve the term *answer,* usually modified by some appropriately descriptive adjective. We shall eventually treat many kinds of answers: answers which are only partial, or which give more information than was asked for, or which are logically equivalent to direct answers without being direct answers, or which correct a false presupposition of the question, etc. All these fall within the province of erotetic logic, but, equally, all must be distinguished from direct answers.

1.2 Elementary Questions   In this section and the next we shall be concerned with the dual task of providing an analytical set of concepts with which to talk about elementary questions and their answers, and some notation for asking and answering questions which reflects that analysis. (Notation cannot of course be an independent source of illumination.)

   The notation for a question is called an *interrogative formula* or *sentence* (depending on whether or not it contains free variables), which we here shorten to just *interrogative.* An interrogative is said to *put* a question. Because two interrogative sentences may put the same question, and for other reasons as well, one should articulate the concept of a question as something more abstract than a piece of notation, and one should distinguish questions from interrogatives. We shall try to be as careful as we can in maintaining the distinction, but we shall be somewhat more relaxed in speaking of examples drawn from ordinary discourse than when speaking of our formal language L.

Our strategy will be to introduce the notation for interrogatives one part at a time, each part being introduced just after the theoretical analysis of the part of a question on which it depends. In cases where questions and interrogatives have matching parts to which it is convenient to give the same name, we shall use the adjective *abstract* for the part of the question, and *lexical* for the part of interrogative, with the understanding that these adjectives may be dropped whenever context makes it clear which is intended. The abstract part of the question will also be said to *belong,* derivatively, to the interrogative.

We think the concept of direct answer fundamental to any fruitful theory of questions. (As Åqvist has so thoroughly and elegantly demonstrated, however, much is possible without using the notion in any official way.) For erotetic logic, however, it is not enough to say that a statement is an answer to a question; one must also say how a statement answers its question. Securing this further refinement of the notion of direct answer requires preliminary elucidation of questions. A question, on our account, consists of two parts to which we attach the artificial names *abstract subject* and *abstract request.* It is the subjects of questions which will concern us in the remainder of section 1.2.

A first approximation to the central idea is that each question is to be conceived as presenting a range of alternatives as its subject, from among which alternatives the respondent is to make a selection as from a tray of hors d'oeuvres. For example, we may think of the question

(2)   *Is glass a liquid at 70°F.?*

as presenting as its subject the two alternatives

(3)   *Glass is a liquid at 70°F.*

and "*Glass is not a liquid at 70° F.*" Similarly, "*Does brass contain more copper than tin or more tin than copper?*" presents the two alternatives "*Brass contains more copper than tin*" and "*Brass contains more tin than copper.*" But (1) presents infinitely many alternatives, "*The freezing point of water under standard conditions is 0° F.,*" "*The freezing point of water under standard conditions is 1° F.,*" and so on, as well as subzero analogues of these.

The point is obvious, but nevertheless our treatment of a question as presenting a range of alternatives as its subject is to be contrasted with one which would conceive the glass question as presenting as its subject the single proposition "*Glass is a liquid at 70° F.*" and requesting the respondent's assent thereto or denial thereof. It is a fact that this other view, shared by perhaps most of those older logicians who thought and wrote about questions, has not led to a viable erotetic logic. The chief limitation of the older theory lies in its wrongful overemphasis on the "yes-no" question at the expense of overlooking a large array of other sorts. For although conceiving questions as presenting a single proposition for assent or denial works well for the simple yes-no case, it turns out to be difficult or impossible to generalize to more complex cases. The limitation is, indeed, exactly analogous to that which the Aristotelian logician laid on himself by overemphasis on the categorical proposition and perhaps is what some persons wrongly put by saying that logic is not "really" two-valued.

Questions present alternatives as their subject and also determine their direct answers, but the concepts are not the same. There are pairs of questions, such as "*Which primes lie between 10 and 20?*" and "*What's an example of a prime lying between 10 and 20?*", which are alike in the alternatives they present but which differ in the answers they require. It follows that there is more to a question than its subject. We defer until section 1.3 determination of the nature of this something more, which we will call the question's "request," and we will continue now with an examination of some of the consequences of conceiving the subject of a question as a presentation of alternatives.

Questions can be classified into two sorts with respect to how many alternatives they present: a few, or at any rate a finite number of alternatives, on the one hand, and an infinite, or at least a large number of alternatives, on the other. The division between the finite and infinite cases is of course interesting and important, but for present purposes we shall look not at how many alternarives are present but rather at the *manner* of their presentation. Either the alternatives are explicitly listed in the question or else they are described by reference to some condition or matrix, where a *condition* or *matrix* is a statement form with variables holding the place of names. For example, the alternatives in the brass question are explicitly listed in the question, but the infinitely many alternatives presented by (1) are presented by reference to the matrix, "*The freezing point of water under standard conditions is $x°F$.*" And this distinction leads to a first principle of classification of questions: whether-questions vs. which-questions. This division is not exhaustive, but we may for convenience stipulate that the class of *elementary* questions is exhausted by these two sorts, and we will take up each in turn.

1.21 Whether-questions; Their Subjects Some questions present as their *abstract subject* a finite set of alternatives, this set being explicitly contained in the questions. Such we call *whether-questions.* Ordinary yes-no questions such as (2) are whether-questions, for from the question we can easily and directly recover the statements presented as alternatives. Another example is King James I's question,

(4)   *Tobacco smoking: a vice, a virtue, a vagary, an extravagance, a cure for all ills?*

the subject of which is constituted by five alternatives, the first two of which are "*Tobacco smoking is a vice*" and "*Tobacco smoking is a virtue.*" Any finite set of formulas is called an *abstract whether-subject,* and it is fit to be the abstract subject of a whether-question. The *range determined by* a whether-subject of a whether-question, i.e., the set of *alternatives* it *presents,* is defined as identical with its subject. This identification will no longer hold good for which-questions, the ranges of which are distinct from their subjects.

Notation: Since an elementary question is constituted by its subject and request, we shall want interrogatives putting elementary questions to reflect this fact, and if we think of the question mark as signifying that function which takes a request and a subject as its arguments and produces a question as its value, we can hardly escape taking the common pattern of all elementary interrogatives to be $?\rho\sigma$. The choice of order for the request ρ and the subject σ is indeterminate on logical grounds, but considerations of readability which do not emerge for some time suggest the ρ-σ ordering.

Determination of what should be put for the lexical subject in the case of whether-interrogatives begins in the reflection that the abstract subject of a whether-question is a set of statements

(5) $\{A_1, \ldots, A_n\}$

So, obviously, the most serviceable lexical subject is obtained by writing a list of the alternatives (5), separated by commas, the whole to be enclosed in parentheses. Given formulas $A_1, \ldots, A_n$, we shall therefore say that

(6) $\quad (A_1, \ldots, A_n)$

is a *lexical whether-subject.* For fussy technical reasons, we shall require that there be no repetitions among $A_1, \ldots, A_n$; clearly no generality is thereby lost. For even fussier reasons, we also require that no one of the A_i of either (5) or (6) be a conjunction $A_{i_1} \,\&\, \ldots \,\&\, A_{i_p}$ of other of the A_j, thus ruling out $(C, A, B, A\&B)$–but not $(A, A\&B)$. This would cost us generality were it not for the availability of gramatically distinct but logically equivalent ways of expressing $A_{i_1} \,\&\, \ldots \,\&\, A_{i_p}$, e.g., via its own double negation. Our reasons, incidentally, have nothing to do with the usefulness of questions with subjects like $(A, B, A\&B)$. Indeed, such subjects have their uses, but in any event it is not the job of the logician to reject an erotetic form just because someone who used it would ordinarily be doing something silly. What we secure by this requirement is that if a formula $S_1 \,\&\, \ldots \,\&\, S_p$ can be construed as a conjunction of some among the A_i, then it can be so construed in exactly one way, something which later turns out to have a point.

It follows that interrogatives putting whether-questions can be identified by the pattern

(7) $\quad ?\rho(A_1, \ldots, A_n)$

We shall say that the lexical whether-subject (6) is the *subject of* (7), and that (7) is a *whether-interrogative.*

The lexical whether-subject (6) is said to *signify* the abstract whether-subject (5). Since (5) determines a range, i.e., a set of alternatives, we shall also say that (6) and (7) determine this range and present those alternatives via their connection with (5). (These ways of speaking will be more useful in the case of which-questions. We introduce them now for uniformity.)

Examples: Let L abbreviate (3). Then the interrogative putting (2) would have the form $?\rho(L, \bar{L})$, which is the canonical pattern for "proper" yes-no questions. Let B be "*John used to beat his wife*" and N be "*John does not now beat his wife.*" Then the most plausible construction to put on

(8)   *Has John stopped beating his wife?*

is undoubtedly by way of an interrogative $?\rho(B\&N, B\&\bar{N})$, which is the canonical pattern for "improper" yes-no questions, i.e., those exhibiting the badly named "fallacy of many questions." And the interrogative for King James's tobacco question (4) would have the form $?\rho(A_1, A_2, A_3, A_4, A_5)$.

1.22   Which-questions; Their Subjects; Real and Nominal Alternatives
As a first approximation, which-questions are those that present their alternatives by reference to a matrix and one or more category conditions. For example,

(9)   *Which positive integer is the smallest prime greater than 45?*

presents infinitely many alternatives by reference to the matrix

(10)   *x is the smallest prime greater than 45*

and the category condition

(11)   *x is a positive integer.*

In section 1.0 we postulated that with each category condition there are associated two distinct sets: first a set of names (e.g., the Arabic numerals "1", "2", etc.) and second a set of entities (e.g., the set of positive integers). In section 1.0 the set of names associated with a category condition was called a *nominal* category, while the set of associated entities was called a *real* category. This doubling of concepts permeates our treatment of which-questions; it corresponds to the way in which one vacillates between the numeral "47" and the number 47 as defining what one "really" wants in asking (9). Were the denotation function of semantics both one-one and onto, we would not need both sets. But it is not in general one-one, since two names can denote the same entity, e.g., both "3^2" and "9" denote 9, and it is not in general onto, since in any given interpretation there may be nameless entities, e.g., since there are more real numbers than names, any given interpretation for ordinary mathematics will have real numbers in its domain which, in that interpretation, have no name. We recall that the two sets are connected by our requirement that in an interpretation it must be the case for each category condition that the denotations of names in its nominal category fall within its real category, as the denotation of each Arabic numeral is an integer.

The distinction between two types of category leads to a distinction between two types of alternatives, which we may call respectively *nominal* and *real alternatives*, of which both sorts play roles in erotetic logic. The nominal alternatives presented by (9) are defined as all and only the results of substituting members of the nominal category determined by the category condition (11), i.e., non-"0" Arabic numerals, for the variable x in the matrix (10). Thus, the nominal alternatives presented by (11) are "*1 is the smallest prime greater than 45,"* "*2 is the smallest prime greater than 45,*" etc. This set of nominal alternatives is called the *nominal range* of (9).

The real alternatives presented by (9) cannot be defined in terms of substitution, since, of course, it makes no sense to substitute a nonlinguistic entity for the variable x in (10). We may, however, obtain the desired effect by defining real alternatives presented by (9) as ordered pairs ⟨f, "*x is the smallest prime greater than 45*"⟩, where f is a function which assigns to the variable x some entity in the real category associated with (11), i.e., the positive integers. We may think of such an ordered pair as a proposition affirming that the entity $f(x)$ assigned by f to x satisfies the matrix (10), and we may call it "true" or "false" according as $f(x)$ does or does not satisfy (10). The set of all such alternatives is called the *real range* of (9).

The function f does not have much work to do in the above example, since we are interested in only one of its values: $f(x)$. It begins to come into its own only when we generalize to make room for "relational" which-questions such as

(12)   *Which boys are brothers of which girls?*,

which employs a two-place matrix

(13)   *x is a brother of y*,

together with a pair of category conditions, one for each place,

(14)   *x is a boy*, and *y is a girl*.

The nominal range of (12) will consist in the various sentences obtainable by substituting boy's names for x and girls' names for y in the matrix (13), while the real range will consist in the various pairs ⟨*f*, "*x is a brother of y*"⟩, where *f*(*x*) is a boy and *f*(*y*) a girl.*

In order to generalize further in such a way that we will later have convenient ways of talking about "question-schemata" such as

(15)   *What is the solution of a+x = b?*,

it is useful to reflect in our terminology those variables of a matrix like "*a*+*x* = *b*" which are queried (here, clearly, *x*) and those which are not (here, *a* and *b*). We shall call such queried variables *queriables*. It is the queriables which are "erotetically bound," neither bound to an ordinary assertoric quantifier, nor free, but bound to the interrogative itself.

A suitable generalization should also leave open the possibility of omitting category conditions governing some or all of the queriables of a matrix, for sometimes the limitations on alternatives arising therefrom may be unnecessary or undesirable. And it should have built into it the fact that category conditions differing only in their variables are equivalent. We therefore introduce the idea of a "category mapping" in a set of queriables *X* by defining a function *g* as a *category mapping in X* if *g* is a mapping from a (perhaps empty) subset of *X* into the set of equivalence classes of category conditions. The idea is that where *g*(*x*) is undefined, *x* is to be free of category restrictions, while if *g*(*x*) is defined, *x* is to be governed by any arbitrarily chosen category condition chosen from the set *g*(*x*) of equivalent conditions.

---

*Ranier Lang (correspondence, 1970) reports that relational which questions hardly ever occur in natural language, and are not very well understood when they do: "My attempts at trying out relational which-questions on our New Guineans proved utter failures." But the analogy with assertoric logic nevertheless suggests they should be of a high order of importance in serious scientific communication.

In the general case, we shall therefore need three items to determine the real and nominal alternatives presented by a which-question. A. a set of queriables, X; B. a category mapping in X, g; and C. a matrix, A. Provided that X is non-empty, we define an *abstract which-subject* as a triple $\langle X, g, A \rangle$ consisting of these three items.* It will be recalled from section 1.21 that in the case of whether-questions, the abstract whether-subject is the same as the range of alternatives, but for which-questions the two are not to be identified. This reflects our decision to say that if two which-questions with different subjects, as defined above, happened in some odd case to present the same set of alternatives, as defined below, they would still be two.

The appropriate definitions for alternatives presented by which-questions are these. Let the triple

(16) $\langle X, g, Ax_1 \ldots x_n \rangle$

be a which-subject, where, as required, X is a nonempty set $\{x_1, \ldots, x_n\}$ of queriables, g is a category mapping in X, and $Ax_1 \ldots x_n$ is a matrix. Then the *nominal alternatives* making up the *nominal range determined by* this which-subject and *presented* by any question with this subject are the results $Aa_1 \ldots a_n$ of substituting a name a_i for a queriable x_i (each i) in the matrix $Ax_1 \ldots x_n$, subject to the restriction that if $g(x_i)$ is defined and is the equivalence class of category conditions Cx, then a_i must be in the nominal category determined by Cx.

---

*This is wrong, because it makes $(x \mathbin{//} Fx)$ and $(y \mathbin{//} Fy)$ (see paragraph under display 19) signify distinct abstract subjects in spite of the fact that since x and y are bound, they ought to signify identical abstract subjects. What is wanted instead of $\langle X, g, A \rangle$ is something amounting to the equivalence-class generated from this by means of uniform substitution for queriables. Alas, we caught this mistake too late to make the necessary changes.

The real range, being semantic, must be relativized to interpretations. For an interpretaion M, the *real M-alternatives,* or
alternatives in M, which make up the *real M-range* or *range in
M, determined by* (16) and *presented by* any question with
this subject are defined as all the pairs $\langle f, Ax_1 \ldots x_n \rangle$, with f
a function from the set of queriables X into the domain of
individuals of M, subject to this restriction: if $g(x_i)$ is defined
and is the equivalence class of category conditions Cx, then
$f(x_i)$ is in the real range in M of Cx. A real M-alternative
$\langle f, Ax_1 \ldots x_n \rangle$ is said to be *true in M* just in case $Ax_1 \ldots x_n$
is true in that M' which is like M except in assigning $f(x_i)$ to
x_i, each i. Real and nominal alternatives are connected by the
following definition: with M an interpretation, then relative
to a set of queriables $\{x_1, \ldots, x_n\}$ and a matrix $Ax_1 \ldots x_n$,
the nominal alternative $Aa_1 \ldots a_n$ obtained by substituting
a_i for x_i (each i) *signifies in M* the real alternative $\langle f, Ax_1 \ldots$
$x_n \rangle$, provided that for each i, the name a_i denotes in M the
individual $f(x_i)$. Our assumptions about real and nominal
categories in 1.0 guarantee that if $Aa_1 \ldots a_n$ is a nominal
alternative presented by a subject (16), then if $Aa_1 \ldots a_n$
signifies in M a real alternative $\langle f, Ax_1 \ldots x_n \rangle$ relative to X
and $Ax_1 \ldots x_n$, then the real alternative will be one pre-
sented by the which-subject in M. For example, relative to the
one-member set of queriables $\{x\}$ and the matrix (10), the
nominal alternative *"53 is the smallest prime greater than 45"*
signifies, in the principal interpretation, the real alternative
$\langle f, $ *"x is the smallest prime greater than 45"*$\rangle$, where $f(x) = 53$.

Notation: In section 1.21 we easily found an appropriate
notation for whether-subjects, and finding a suitable parallel
notation for which-subjects is at this stage hardly more difficult. As we have said, an abstract which-subject (16) is con-

stituted by a set of queriables, a category-mapping in this set, and a matrix. There are many pieces of notation from which one could unambiguously recover an abstract which-subject and which would hence be suitable for a lexical which-subject. We have tried most of them. The one we present here seems both compact and readable: we define a *lexical which-subject* as an expression

(17) $(C_1 x_1, \ldots, C_r x_r, x_{r+1}, \ldots, x_n \; // \; A x_1 \ldots x_n)$

subject to the following provisos: $x_1, \ldots, x_n$ is a nonempty nonrepeating sequence of variables $(1 \leqslant n)$, and $C_1 x_1, \ldots, C_r x_r$ is a possibly empty sequence of category conditions such that each $C_1 x_1$ $(1 \leqslant i \leqslant r)$ is a category condition containing x_i as its sole free variable. The idea is that $x_1, \ldots, x_n$ shall be the whole set of queriables, and that the first r of these, which appear free inside the category conditions $C_1 x_1, \ldots, C_r x_r$, shall be those governed by category conditions. Of course, and this is a definition, x_i is to be *governed by* the category condition $C_i x_i$ in which it appears free, while $x_{r+1}, \ldots, x_n$, which stand alone, are said to be *category-free*.

Interrogatives putting which-questions, *which-interrogatives*, then have the form

(18) $?\rho(C_1 x_1, \ldots, C_r x_r, x_{r+1}, \ldots, x_n \; // \; A x_1 \ldots x_n),$

or in the special case where all queriables are category-free, the form

(19) $?\rho(x_1, \ldots, x_n \; // \; A x_1 \ldots x_n).$

Interrogatives having the form (19) are said to be *category-free*.

Given (17), we recover the abstract which-subject (16) it *signifies* as follows: its set of queriables X is the set of variables appearing free to the left of the double virgule; its category mapping is that function g, such that g is defined for exactly those x_i governed by one of the category conditions $C_1 x_1, \ldots, C_r x_r$, and for such an x_i, $g(x_i)$ is the equivalence class $\mathbf{C_i x_i}$ of the category condition $C_i x_i$ governing x_i; and its matrix A is the formula appearing to the right of the double virgule.

All of the various entities we have defined will be said to be *of* one another or to *determine* one another in plausible contexts: (16) and (17) are respectively the abstract and lexical subjects of (18); (17) and (18) determine real and nominal ranges, present real and nominal alternatives, and have a set of queriables, a category mapping and set of category conditions, and a matrix, the converse relationship being expressed in phrases like "the queriables of (18)."

Examples: For (1) we might use the subject (*x is an integer* // *the freezing point of water under standard conditions is $x°F$.*). Here the appropriate category condition "*x is an integer*" needs supplying, and we make the question more precise by filling this lacuna. On the other hand, (12) itself contains phrases suggesting that an appropriate subject might be (*x is a boy, y is a girl* // *x is a brother of y*). One might, however, either prefer or think the sense of the question better given by a category-free subject (*x* // *x is a boy* & *y is a girl* & *x is a brother of y*). Our scheme does not dictate how it is to be used, nor which formal interrogatives best express the meaning of a given English interrogative, being in that respect like formal assertoric logic. We can only suggest plausible alternatives and remark on their differences. For instance, the former subject determines a "smaller" nominal range, comprising only sentences "*b is a brother of c*" with *b* a boy's

name and c a girl's, while the range of the latter includes
every sentence derived from its condition by substitution
with arbitrary names for x and y, including names of horses
and greylag geese. The choice between these might depend on
what the questioner wanted the respondent to canvas in seek-
ing an answer.

Åqvist (1965, p. 164) considers the example *"In what country is Lake Hjälmaren located?"* Our point of view suggests
that the subject of this question is most naturally taken as (x
is a country // Lake Hjälmaren is in x), with *"x is a country"*
taken as a category condition in the obvious way, using, say,
the list of country names of the National Geographic Society
as nominal category. One could also use a category-free variation, putting *"x is a country "* as a conjunct of the matrix instead of as category condition, thus allowing as an alternative
something like *"The native country of Axel Hagerstrom is a
country, and Lake Hjälmaren is in the native country of Axel
Hagerstrom."* Knowing the truth of this would not, of
course, guarantee possessing an answer, in the intuitive sense,
to the question, but Åqvist points out that knowing this and
also knowing the identity of Hagerstrom's native country
would suffice. And it is this latter that he takes as marking an
adequate answer and thus as appropriate to guide his formalization. It seems to us, however, that we increase flexibility
by allowing the questioner to drop the requirement that the
names put for queriables denote individuals known to him, so
that he can frame the question either way, with or without
specifying the knowledge clause. To insist on the clause he
could use the subject, the formal unpacking of which is to be
found in Åqvist, (x *is a country* & *Lake Hjälmaren is in x* &
the questioner knows the identity of x). Then the alternative
obtained by replacing x with the name, *"the native country*

of Axel Hagerstrom," would be false if the questioner did not know the identity of Hagerstrom's native country.*

Finding an appropriate subject for

(20)   *What is the positive square root of π?*

is more complicated. The first thought is to use "$(x^2 = \pi)$ & $(x > 0)$" as the matrix, so that the subject would have the form $(Cx // (x^2 = \pi)$ & $(x > 0))$, but then what category condition should the questioner choose for Cx? Perhaps the questioner knows that the square root of π is some sort of real number, but he does not know that one cannot list names of all the real numbers. In that case, he is likely to choose a category condition whose nominal range is too narrow, omitting a name for the square root of π. If this happens, the respondent should challenge the question, inasmuch as it will have no true answers. On the other hand, the questioner may foolishly choose a category condition that is too wide, including in its nominal range terms such as "$\sqrt{\pi}$" which would yield true but unhelpful answers like *"The square root of π is the square root of π."* A questioner ought, however, to be able to frame a subject determining alternatives which he believes will be helpful if true. That is a cardinal point of the enterprise. In the case of (20), one supposes that what is really wanted is not the square root of π at all, but rather some approximation expressible as a decimal fraction. For example, if we treat (20) as really asking *"What is the positive square root of π, truncated after five decimal places?"*, the appropriate subject would be

*If our assertoric underpinnings included, as do Åqvist's, both an epistemic logic of "knowing that" and a logic free of the classical existential presupposition that every name denotes, then it would be natural to include in our "request" two new "specifications" of the sort discussed in section 3 below, one concerning a "knows the identity" clause and another concerning an existential clause.

(21) $x > 0$ & $\exists y(y$ is an integer & $x = y \times 10^{-5})$
          $// x^2 \leqslant \pi < (x + 10^{-5})^2$.

This illustrates, among other points, the possibility of using complex pieces of notation as category conditions, just so long as a nominal category is specified, in this case, expressions having the form $x_0 . x_1 x_2 x_3 x_4 x_5$, where x_0 is a decimal numeral and the others are decimal digits.

The question

(22)   *Which primeslies between 10 and 20?*

would need as a subject

(23)   (*x is an integer // x is a prime between 10 and 20*).

It might also be plausible to take the subject of (22) as (*x is a prime // x lies between 10 and 20*), but one should be aware that the policy thus enshrined of putting the whole grammatical subject of the English sentence as category conditions of the lexical subject is not always sound. For, by definition, our category conditions are given ahead of time, as part of the definition of the language on a par with what appears in dictionaries and grammar books. Inventing a new category condition is like inventing a new word or a new syntactic construction and, thereby, amounts to a change in the language. The language L permits considerable flexibility in constructing new category conditions out of old, as illustrated in section 1.0, and it contains resources for forming a category condition for every *finite* set $\{a_1, \ldots, a_n\}$ of names via a disjunction $(x = a_1) \vee \ldots \vee (x = a_n)$. But with respect to any fixed language, we cannot make up category conditions as we go along, for they are part of the underlying grammar of the language itself and no more subject to private alteration than are other grammatical features.

Further, an intuitive condition is not going to qualify for formalization as a category condition even via local convention unless the nominal category it intuitively determines is effectively decidable. For example, one cannot take the subject of "*Which theorems of the first order functional calculus contain exactly fourteen symbols?*" to be (*x is a theorem of the first order functional calculus // x contains just fourteen symbols*), since the candidate nominal range, i.e., the set containing all and only names (of a certain style) of theorems of the first-order functional calculus, is not decidable.

To ask a question whose subject determines no true alternatives because of a conflict between category conditions and matrix is to make a *category mistake,* a concept which is ordinarily interesting only if relativized to a set of "meaning postulates" or their equivalent. For example, one would make a category mistake, relative to the usual arithmetical assumptions, by asking "*What are the rational roots of $x^2 = 2?$*" with the understood subject (*x is a rational number // x^2 = 2*). Erotetic logic, however, generates another concept of category mistake: to reply to a question with something that is very like one of the presented alternatives except that names have been substituted in the matrix which are not of the right category, is another sort of category mistake, and the one which is the most interesting. Here the relativization is to the question. Given "*What's an example of something not triangular?*", understood as having (*x is a physical object // x is not triangular*) as its subject, the reply "*Virtue is not triangular*" would be a category mistake. But that same reply would be a perfectly suitable alternative given the category-free subject (*x // x is not triangular*). Again we stress flexibility.

Our general point of view on these examples is that we are unwilling to defend any particular reading we offer of an

English question, on the grounds that such questions are more
often than not ambiguous as to subject, especially as to what
category conditions are to be used. Rather, we wish only to
defend the worth of these concepts and notations in articulating proposed readings with accuracy and flexibility. It is
perhaps worth pointing out that when the data base to be
queried is highly articulated, that articulation itself will generally serve as an appropriate categorization, almost forcing
one to an appropriate set of category conditions.

In any event, although we think the category apparatus
provides a certain amount of illumination of English, that is
not its primary point. Its purpose is as part of a good erotetic
logic, one which is flexible and easy to use and gives the
questioner the kind of control he needs in order to be able to
ask the precise question he wants to.

1.3 Answers and Questions   A direct answer is a statement, so
that, like any statement, it can be seen from the point of view
of ordinary assertoric logic as having a certain logical form.
Beyond this, however, it will be seen by erotetic logic as
having additional form when taken in relation to questions to
which it supplies an answer, for in order to understand fully
an answer to a question, one must do more than understand
barely that it is an answer, one must also understand how it
is an answer. According to the present analysis, how a direct
answer answers an elementary question has three aspects or
parts: the selection, the completeness-claim, and the distinctness-claim. The selection consists of those alternatives which
the answer selects from among the alternatives presented by
the question. The completeness-claim of an answer refers to
the degree of completeness of its selection as measured against
the whole set of true alternatives. And the distinctness-claim

refers to whether or not distinct nominal alternatives stand
for distinct real alternatives. This capsule account of answers
is expanded below.

As for questions, we rely on Hamblin's dictum (1958):
"Knowing what counts as an answer is equivalent to knowing
the question." On this insight rests the whole of our erotetic
logic: the essence of a question is the way in which it determines its direct answers, so that from the question it is possible for the participants in an erotetic situation to tell what
the direct answers are to be. Were we awarding no internal
structure to direct answers, it would be plausible to identify
this "essence" of a question with the set of its direct answers.
The results of our analysis suggest, however, that it will be
fruitful to permit determination of direct answers to be
mediated by way of selection, completeness-claim, and
distinctness-claim. Following up this line of thought, we suggest that every elementary question is sufficiently described
by setting forth first its subject, as described in section 1.2,
and second the specifications it lays down concerning the
form of the three parts of its direct answers. According to
one metaphor, a question presents a range of alternatives via
its subject and then "requests" that the respondent concoct
some sort of direct answer therefrom, so that with nothing
more than this picture in mind we choose to call the second
part of a question its *request.* According to another and less
polite metaphor, the job of the "request" part of a question
is to lay down blueprints specifying the form which each of
the three parts of a direct answer must take, so that we
choose to call *specifications* the three parts of the request
corresponding to the three parts of direct answers. We will
take up in turn in sections 1.31–1.33 the three parts of a
direct answer and the correlative three specifications making

up a question's request. In these sections we shall often say just "answer" instead of the more proper "direct answer". No ambiguity can result, since we shall be dealing in these sections with direct answers, to the exclusion of any other kind.

We call attention here to a certain mild incoherence in our analysis which we have seen fit to accept: as indicated in our discussion of coded answers in section 1.1, we insist that the assertoric meaning of answers be context independent. But we are going to define things in such a way that the erotetic meaning of an answer—its "how"—is dependent on the interrogative to which it is taken as an answer. The only way to avoid this would be to require the interrogative itself, or at least some part of it, to be (physically) part of each answer thereto, which, in spite of its enormous formal convenience, we think too heavy a price. The upshot is that a formula which can be taken as answering one interrogative in one way can also be taken as answering a different interrogative in a different way. But for a fixed interrogative, an answer's way of answering that interrogative is uniquely determined (*univocity*).

1.31 Selection and Selection-Size Specification   The first of three parts of a direct answer is its *selection*: a direct answer provides an answer to its question partly by selecting some subset of the alternatives presented by the question, claiming (rightly or wrongly) that the selected alternatives are one and all true. Every direct answer to every question makes such a selection and such a claim, so that just as with every question there is correlated a range of presented alternatives, so with every direct answer there is correlated a selection of alternatives. In the case of answers to which-questions, the real-vs-nominal distinction yields two sorts of selection: the *nominal selection,* which contains nominal alternatives, and the *real selection,* which is a function of this, namely, the set of real alternatives signified by members of the nominal selection relative to the queriables and satisfaction-condition of its subject.

Often a direct answer selects exactly one alternative, but not always. This is one of the reasons that alternatives and direct answers must be kept separate. As answers to (22) we should construe the false direct answer

(24)   *13 alone is a prime lying between 10 and 20*

as selecting exactly one alternative, while the equally false answer

(25)   *13 and 17 alone are primes lying between 10 and 20*

has a selection of cardinality two. And, of course, the true direct answer to (22) should be construed as selecting exactly four of the alternatives presented via the subject (23). To some questions we may construe the response "None" as a selection of the empty subset of alternatives, but that, as we shall see, depends on the question

Every alternative selected must be one of those presented by the question via its subject, and exercising this control over selections is one of the chief functions of the subject. But the question controls not only the content but also the size of the selections of its answers. It does this through the first component of its request, the *selection-size specification.* Consider together the example (22) and the question

(26)   *Which prime lies between 10 and 20?*

It seems to us fruitful to construe (22) and (26) as having exactly the same subject, viz., (23), but in spite of this identity of subject, the questions are evidently different. To see this, note that (24) and (25), although false, are both direct answers to (22), while (25) is not a direct answer to (26), since (26) specifies that its direct answers must select a single alternative, not two. In contrast to (26), the selection-size specification of (22) allows direct answers with selections of arbitrary cardinality except zero—"except zero" provided (22), which we think mildly ambiguous, is read as not allowing the empty selection represented in English by "None." We shall therefore say that (26) as well as its cousin

(27)   *What's an example of a prime lying between 10 and 20?*

makes a request employing the *single alternative selection-size specification,* while (22) and

(28)   *What are some of the primes lying between 10 and 20?*

employ the *almost nonlimiting selection-size specification*— "almost," since selections of cardinality zero are excluded. The (absolutely) *nonlimiting selection-size specification,* which entitles a respondent to make his selection of any size whatsoever, including zero, is unambiguously employed in the request made by

(29)   *Which primes lie between 10 and 20, or aren't there any?*

A selection-size specification controls the size of the selection, but not every sort of control is of distinctively erotetic interest. One can imagine sound reasons based on information processing aspects of the erotetic situation for wanting just one alternative, or a few alternatives, or between 20 and

40 alternatives, but it is hard to see what generally applicable erotetic consideration could lead us to want, say, an even number of alternatives.* We therefore settle on taking the lower limit as fully representing any selection-size specification, and we explicitly include cases, like the almost non-limiting specification, which put no upper limit. Justifying this last sort of specification is particularly easy, for we shall want to use it whenever we want a complete list of all the true alternatives, however many there be. Precisely in that case we cannot put an upper limit on how many we will accept. But, it may be asked, why should we ever wish to make a more limited sort of specification? Both the upper limit and the lower limit must be justified. The answer, or part of it, for the upper limit is that we may wish to restrict the number of selected alternatives for either of two reasons. First, knowing that there are many true alternatives, we may want to keep the number of selected alternatives below a certain level in order to avoid excessive payment to the respondent if we must pay him for his answers, or in any case to avoid unjustifiable use of his time and energy. Indeed, we may wish to avoid answers of such length that it would be inconvenient, inefficient, or impossible for us to process them. Asking for a thousand articles on the genetics of hemophilia may not be as useful as asking for two or three, and this for reasons intrinsic to the erotetic enterprise itself, viewed as one information processor facing another. Second, we may wish to use the selection-size specification as a device for giving the respon-

---

*In special circumstances where one would need (say) an even number of alternatives, one would expect that the underlying assertoric language would have enough power to express this fact so that it could be made part of the subject. We wish to include in our "requests" only specifications which are "topic-neutral" in the way that the connectives and quantifiers of assertoric logic are topic-neutral.

dent information useful to him in finding the desired answer with a minimum of wasted effort. Consider

(29′)   *What are the freezing points of water, in degrees Fahrenheit, under standard conditions?*

If we were to ask (29′) of a stupid enough respondent, he might go on and on, even after finding that 32 satisfies the condition, endlessly testing all the integers, consulting encyclopedias, or running experiments in a vain attempt to find other entries for a complete list. If a questioner, however, knowing that there is but one freezing point of water in degrees Fahrenheit under standard conditions but not knowing what it is, were to use the single-alternative specification as in (1), then the respondent would know, upon finding that 32 satisfies the condition, that he had found the materials from which to construct an adequate direct answer. And he would know this not via any logical or physical expertise, but just by understanding the form of the question.

For a similar pair of reasons, one might want to put a lower limit on the size of the selection, in order to obtain, e.g., a sufficiently large sample for purposes of the questioner, or in order to give the respondent some idea of how much work he is going to have to do.

There is plausibility in the suggestion (Åqvist 1965, p. 161) that we need only a lower limit, counting replies which select alternatives beyond that number as superfluous, i.e., as really giving more information than the questioner wanted, since the form of his question anyhow suggests that he is going to be entirely satisfied with an answer, the selection of which meets the lower limit exactly. We therefore need to justify our provision for a range of selection size. For example, why would a questioner ever want "between three and five" alternatives instead of "at least three"? The situation we have in mind may be described in economic terms as follows. (a) The questioner must have at least three alternatives for his purposes, and is therefore unwilling to pay for or bother with a reply containing fewer than three alternatives. (b) Three he finds helpful, so he will pay for three, but (c) four or five would be better, and he would be willing to pay extra for the extra information imparted by the fourth and fifth. Lastly, (d) five is enough, so he is unwilling to pay for alternatives beyond the fifth. In these circumstances, he should ask a question making the "between three and five" selection-size specification rather than the "exactly three" or the "at least three" specification. From the point of view of utility theory, the case may also be described by saying that the questioner's utility function, which measures the value of information conveyed to him by various numbers of alternatives, is such that it gives the value 0 to answers with fewer than three alternatives, is strictly increasing between three and five, and is level after five. Since there is usually a cost for processing extra alternatives, he will want a cutoff after five.

Notation: In section 1.2 we introduced the notation $?\rho\sigma$ for interrogatives, specializing this to (7) and (18) in sections 1.21 and 1.22 respectively. We have as yet no notation at all for answers. We now add notational conventions of the following three kinds: A. Since we have determined the first part of a direct answer as a selection, we describe the notation relevant thereto. B. Similarly, we introduce notation reflecting the matching selection-size specification of the interrogative. C. We define the relevant question-answer relationships, laying down the grammatical conditions under which a selection can be part of a direct answer to an interrogative as determined by the subject and selection-size specification of the latter.

A. Direct answers are going to have, as a first approximation, three conjuncts, thus having the form *S&C&D,* where *S* is the selection, *C* the completeness-claim, and *D* the distinctness-claim. It will turn out that either one or both of *C* and *D* can be missing, but never the selection *S*, so that it is more exact to say that direct answers have one of the forms

(30)   *S&C&D, S&C, S&D, S*

Since the first part of every answer is a selection of alternatives, with a claim that all are true, we represent *S* quite simply as a conjunction

(31) $S_1 \& \ldots \& S_p$

of the desired alternatives, assuming for convenience that in the case of whether-questions there are no repetitions among $S_1, \ldots, S_p$. (31) is said to be a *selection.* In the case of which-questions, the *nominal selection signified by* (31) is the set

(32) $\{S_1, \ldots, S_p\},$

and if each of $S_1, \ldots, S_p$ is in the range of a which-subject σ, then *the real selection signified by* (31) *in M relative to* σ is defined as the set of real alternatives signified by the members of (32) in *M* relative to σ. Occasionally we shall say that (31) is a *lexical* and (32) an *abstract selection.* The form of direct answers is now seen to be

(33) $(S_1 \& \ldots \& S_p)\&C\&D,$

or a variation missing *C* or *D,* and (31), (32), and the signified nominal and real selections are said to be *of* (33).

B. We now come to the specification of ρ in $?\rho\sigma$. Every request has three parts, the selection-size specification, the completeness-claim specification, and the distinctness-claim specification, so that we shall render the request ρ as

(34)   (*s c d*),

thus giving interrogatives the form

(35)   ?(*s c d*)σ.

The first part of the request, represented by *s*, is the selection-size specification, which by our analysis sets upper and lower limits on the size of selections. It seems most memorable to employ for it a pair of numerals signifying those limits, using up-down to indicate which is which: $\frac{u}{v}$. The lower numeral v and the upper numeral u represent respectively the lower and upper limits of admissible selection sizes. The lower numeral v should in spirit be a nonnegative numeral 0, 1, . . . , but so as to spare ourselves some technical complexities that would arise in the case of empty selections, we disallow 0, requiring that v be replaced by a positive numeral 1, 2, 3, ... The upper numeral must be greater than or equal to the lower. We shall let u be replaced by a dash when we wish to indicate that no upper limit is being set: $\frac{-}{v}$. An inscription like $\frac{5}{3}$ then signifies the between-three-and-five selection-size specification, while $\frac{-}{3}$ specifies that the number of alternatives selected in any direct answer must be at least three, without upper limit. The single-alternative selection-size specification is signified by $\frac{1}{1}$, while the almost nonlimiting specification is given by $\frac{-}{1}$.

We shall say of such notation that it is a *lexical selection-size specification,* and that it *signifies* the corresponding *abstract selection-size specification,* which may be thought of as an ordered pair of cardinals (or the dash) subject to conditions analogous to those above.

Putting this new notation in its place makes requests look like

(36) $(^u_v \, c \, d)$

and interrogatives look like

(37) $?(^u_v \, c \, d)\sigma$.

We shall say that ^u_v and the abstract selection-size specification it signifies are *of* (36) and (37).

C. We now bring together our partial notation for questions and our partial notation for answers by means of some definitions. The first trio shows how the subject and request combine in their influence on answers.

In the first place, we say that a *subject, σ, sanctions* a selection (31) if each of the conjuncts $S_1, \ldots, S_p$ is in the range determined by σ. That is to say, if σ is a whether-subject (6), then each S_j $(1 \leqslant j \leqslant p)$ must be a distinct one of the A_i $(1 \leqslant i \leqslant n)$ and if σ is a which-subject (17), then each S_j must have the form $Ab_1 \ldots b_n$, where each b_i is in the nominal category determined by the category condition, if any, governing x_i.

Second, we say that a *request, ρ, sanctions* a selection (31) if the length p of (31) falls within the limits specified by the selection-size specification of ρ. That is, if ρ is $(^u_v \, c \, d)$, then it is required that $v \leqslant p \leqslant u$, except that if u is a dash, then the only requirement is that $v \leqslant p$.*

---

*Selection-size specifications could have been reified more neatly by letting u be the least cardinal *not* allowed, so that in transfinite generalizations up to some cardinal $\aleph_\alpha$, one would have simply $\aleph_\alpha$ instead of a dash. But that system, though necessary for transfinite generalization, would in the finite case have been considerably less memorable.

Third, we say that an *interrogative, I, sanctions* a selection if both the request and the subject of *I* do; i.e., if *I* is ?*ρσ*, then *I* sanctions (31) if both *ρ* sanctions (31) and *σ* sanctions (31).

The fourth and crucial definition has to be a trifle anticipatory and a trifle partial. One is going to be able to tell from the interrogative which of the forms *S&C&D, S&C, S&D,* or *S* is at issue for a given candidate direct answer *A*, and given this, we will call *S* the selection *of A*. Then—and this is the definition, if only partial—a necessary condition that *A* be a *direct answer to* an interrogative *I* is that *S* be a selection sanctioned by *I*.

These definitions require no comment, being just the formal embodiment of our previous discussion of how subjects and selection-size specifications control the content and form of direct answers.

We have defined sanctioning as between lexical items, but of course one may also think of abstract subjects, abstract requests, and questions as sanctioning abstract selections, of either the nominal or real variety. We omit the details.

Examples: Using "*P(x)*" for "*x is a prime between 10 and 20*," both (26) and (27) would have a form using the single-alternative selection-size specification: ?($^1_1$ *c d*) (*x is an integer* // *P(x)*). They would thus sanction selections "*P(1)*," "*P(6)*," etc., but neither "*P(17) & P(19)*" (wrong selection-size—not sanctioned by request) nor "*P(3/4)*" (sanctioned by request all right, but not by subject—wrong category).

On the other hand, (22) and (28) would have a form using the almost nonlimiting selection-size specification, ?($^-_1$ *c d*) (*x is an integer* // *P(x)*), and thus would sanction every selection sanctioned by the above and selections like "*P(17) &*

$P(19)$" as well. But "$P(3/4)$" would still be a category mistake. In addition to (26) and (27), examples (1), (2), (8), (9), (15), and (20) all should probably be taken as having the form $?(_1^1 \; c \; d)\sigma$, while in addition to (22) and (28), examples (12) and (29′) probably have the form $?(_1^- \; c \; d)\sigma$. The form of (4), with respect to its selection-size specification, seems to us ambiguous, but the reader is invited to argue. Perhaps it was intended as having the form $?(_1^- \; c \; d)$ (*Vice, Virtue, Vagary, Extravagance, Cure*) (where "*Vice*" abbreviates "*Tobacco smoking is a vice*," etc.), thus as using the almost nonlimiting selection-size specification. And precising "few" by "from three to six." we would render "*What are a few cities with populations greater than that of Boston?*" by $?(_3^6 \; c \; d)$ (*x is a city // Population(x) > Population (Boston)*).

Using "$I(x)$" for "*x is an integer*," we could formalize (22) in a category-free way, putting $I(x)$ in the matrix $?(_1^- \; c \; d)$ ($x \; // \; I(x) \& P(x)$). Then the sanctioned selections would be longer, since the matrix is longer: "$I(3)\&P(3)$" (one alternative), "($I(2)\&P(2)$) & ($I(6)\&P(6)$)" (two alternatives), etc. This shows that it is good policy to put conditions in as category conditions whenever possible, rather than as conjuncts of the matrix, so as to cut down on the length of answers.

1.32 *Completeness-claim and Completeness-claim Specification*
The second component of a direct answer, the existence of which is not always obvious from inspection of English examples, is called the *completeness-claim.* Consider the question (drawn from *McGuffey's Reader*)

(38)   *Did you say valor, or value?*

which (making allowance for change in pronouns) we construe as presenting the two alternatives

(39)   *I said valor*

and

(40)   *I said value.*

On intuitive grounds, or because of a desire to stay as close as possible to ordinary English, one might suppose that a "proper" direct answer to (38) would consist simply in the selection of one of the alternatives, e.g., (39). It seems to us, however, that (39) is code for

(41)   *I said valor, and I did not say value,*

the context of utterance making the additional clause, which denies (40), unnecessary. For suppose that the respondent knew that he had said both words. Then surely, if he replied with (39), he would be accused of just as much lack of candor as if he had replied with (41). Indeed, if he knew that he had said both words, he ought not to have directly answered the question at all, but rather replied with "*I said both valor and value*" as a "corrective answer." The point, incidentally, by no means escaped McGuffey: he gives as an answer to (38) the wholly unambiguous sentence, "*I said value, not valor.*"

So there is more to a direct answer than its selection. As further evidence for this contention, think for a moment of (22) as occurring on an examination, and consider the fate of the student who responded with, say

(42)   *11, 13, and 17.*

Evidently this, taken as a code for a full direct answer, is a false answer to (22); and the student who so answers will be marked "wrong," since he has neglected the fact that 19 also satisfies the matrix of (23). Therefore, his list (42) cannot be construed merely as code for a selection

(43)   (*11 is a prime between 10 and 20*) & (*13 is a prime
         between 10 and 20*) & (*17 is a prime between 10 and
         20*),

since (43) is true, while we agreed that the student's list (42)
should be marked "wrong". Rather, as an answer to (22), the
list (42) must be read as doing more than selecting the list of
true alternatives given in (43). It must be read as coding the
additional false claim that the selected alternatives constitute
a complete list of all the true alternatives in the range of (22).
It is just because this further claim to completeness is being
made and is false that we mark the student wrong. Thus, we
should treat (42) as a code for the conjunction of the selection (43) with the following false completeness-claim: "*There
are no primes between 10 and 20 other than, at most, 11, 13,
17.*" We remark that this claim can be recast into a less idiomatic but logically more tractable form: "*Every prime between
10 and 20 is identical to one of 11, 13, and 17,*" which is just
a way of saying that every true alternative is contained in the
selection, i.e., that the selection is a complete list of all the
true alternatives. And exactly the same analysis applies to the
valor-value question (38): the response (39) has the effect of
selecting the "valor" alternative (39) and then adding that
this alternative exhausts the true alternatives in the range of
(38).

  That (22) calls for a completeness-claim on the part of its
answers becomes even more obvious when we contrast it with
(28), which is otherwise just like it except in this particular:
(22) and (28) have identical subjects and identical selection-
size specifications (the almost nonlimiting), but (22) calls for
a completeness-claim while (28) does not. Upon being asked
(28) it would certainly be inappropriate to go beyond a
selection such as (43) in order to make any sort of complete-

ness-claim. (28) asks for examples, and to give a completeness-claim would be to provide more information than is called for by the question, just like the father in Little Rock.

Having become convinced that one should not overlook completeness-claims on the part of answers, it is easy to fall into the opposite error of supposing that every question requests a completeness-claim, and to suppose as a corollary that to every question there is at most one true answer. It is therefore important to realize that the direct answers to (28), and indeed to (27) as well, not only do not but must not make completeness-claims. That this is so can be read off from the questions themselves. We call the second part of the request of a question, which specifies whether or not a completeness-claim is to be made, the *completeness-claim specification,* and though not all answers make completeness-claims, all questions, in order to allow the option, must contain a completeness-claim specification. As terminology, we shall say that (22) and (26) employ the *maximum completeness-claim specification,* which specifies that answers must claim that all true alternatives are in the selection, and that (27) and (28) employ the *empty completeness-claim specification,* which specifies that direct answers are not to make a completeness-claim. To such questions, as to (27) and (28), there is ordinarily a multitude of true direct answers.

There are other sorts of completeness-claims than that to complete exhaustiveness. Let us suppose one wants a 5% sample of secretaries listed in a personnel data file. Then one queries the file with the question, "*Who are 5% of the secretaries listed?*" Any direct answer to this question must of course select a list claimed to be secretaries, but it must also at least implicitly claim that the selection does in fact constitute 5% of the secretaries whose names occur in the file,

thereby making the 5% completeness-claim. Or if one needs a
sample for statistical purposes, one may want neither a complete list of secretaries, nor a fixed number, nor a fixed percentage, but some variable percentage depending on the total
number of secretaries in the file. Here again the selection-size
specification would be almost nonlimiting, but a completeness-claim of a certain kind would be called for.

We now generalize the notion of a completeness-claim as
follows: the completeness-claim made by a direct answer is
always a claim as to how complete the selection is when measured against the totality of true alternatives presented by the
question. That is to say, it is a claim as to how many of the
true alternatives in the range of the question are in the selection of the answer. In this context "how many" is specified
not by a number but by a quantifier such as *all, all but one,*
5%, *most,* etc. Thus, the maximum completeness-claim, the
claim to complete exhaustiveness, is *"All of the true alternatives are in the selection,"* while the 5% completeness-claim is
"5% of true alternatives are in the selection."

In the case of which-questions, the completeness-claim is to
be understood as a claim concerning the degree of completeness of the *real* selection as measured against the total set of
real true alternatives in the real range of the question. And
though in the case of the maximum completeness-claim it
matters little whether the real or nominal *selection* be chosen
here, it is essential that the *total reference* class for quantifiers
used in the maximum completeness-claim be of the real rather
than the nominal variety so as not to convict of falsehood the
man who answers that Cicero was the sole denouncer of
Cataline, when it is also true that Tully (= Cicero) was a
denouncer of Cataline.

The centrality of the notion of the completeness-claim in

our analysis necessitates precision as to what we mean by "quantifier": we define a quantifier Q as a binary relation between classes T (e.g., the set of true alternatives) and S (e.g., the selection), such that whether or not $Q(T, S)$ holds depends entirely on the cardinalities of the intersection $T \cap S$ and the difference T-S of the two sets T and S. (For an alternate and substantially equivalent definition from which this one was derived, see Mostowski 1957).

It would appear that the only quantifiers of fundamental interest in erotetic logic are the "difference-total" quantifiers, i.e., those quantifiers Q such that whether or not $Q(T, S)$ holds depends only on the cardinality of the difference T-S. i.e., $T \cap (-S)$, together with the cardinality of the total reference class T.* The reasonableness of this limitation is suggested by the observation that the degree of completeness of a selection S is best understood in terms of how many of the set of true alternatives T are *left out* of the selection—hence in terms of the cardinality of T-S—when this is measured against the totality of true alternatives, i.e., the cardinality of T. It would seem that the cardinality of the intersection $T \cap S$ has here no role to play, and that "intersection quantifiers" such as the existential quantifier cannot sensibly be employed in making completeness-claims. Accordingly, we shall assume that for the request of a question to specify a form of completeness-claim amounts to specification of either the absence

*Every quantifier can be represented by a set J of ordered pairs of cardinals, the relation between Q and J being the following: $Q(T, S)$ holds if and only if, where i is the cardinality of the intersection $T \cap S$ and d of the difference T-S (i.e., $T \cap (-S)$), the pair $\langle i, d \rangle$ belongs to J. For example, the universal quantifier "all" used in the maximum completeness-claim is represented by the set J such that $\langle i, d \rangle$ belongs to J if and only if $d = 0$, and the "most" quantifier by the set of pairs such that i is greater than d. A difference-total quantifier is recognizable by being represented by a J such that if $\langle i, d \rangle$ belongs to J, then so does every $\langle i', d' \rangle$ such that $d' = d$ and the total $i'+d'$ is the same as the total $i+d$.

of a completeness-claim or of a difference-total quantifier,
and that every *abstract* (as opposed to lexical) *completeness-
claim specification* other than the empty one can be represented by such a quantifier. In contrast to the situation prevailing in the case of selection-size specification, no profit
seems derivable from identifying a completeness-claim specification with a range of quantifiers instead of a single quantifier; however, if we were to introduce sets of quantifiers, the
empty completeness-claim would naturally be represented by
the empty set.

It is doubtless the case that not all difference-total quantifiers represent erotetically interesting completeness-claims.
For example, one would find useless those quantifiers which
make distinctions between various grades of infinity. It is
possible that a natural subset can be defined which will make
a plausible claim to being *the* set of quantifiers representing
completeness-claims, but lack of more definite information
on this head is one reason that we confine our attention in
the remainder of this essay to just one quantifier and one
form of completeness-claim: the universal quantifier, representing the maximum completeness-claim. Another reason for
this limitation is that the assertoric language underlying our
study is possessed of only limited powers of quantificational
expression, so that it seems best to choose quantifiers on the
erotetic side which fall well within these capabilities.

Notation: In order to account for completeness-claims in
our notation, we must A. describe notation by which answers
can make completeness-claims, B. provide notation for completeness-claim specifications for interrogatives, and C. define
the appropriate relations between the two sorts of notation.

A. Direct answers, it will be recalled, have one of the forms

(30) $S\&C\&D, S\&C, S\&D, S,$

where S is the selection, C is the completeness-claim, and D is the distinctness-claim. We have in this section seen why the completeness-claim must be sometimes present and sometimes absent. C, when present, might in the general case have one of many forms, but we have restricted ourselves to only the maximum completeness-claim of the universal quantifier. Since completeness-claims in general, and the maximum claim in particular, have meaning only in relation to the subject of a question or interrogative and will be a function of both that subject, σ, and the selection, S, we can represent the general form of answers making completeness-claims by

(44) $S \ \& \ f(\sigma, S) \ \& \ D$, or $S \ \& \ f(\sigma, S)$,

where f is determined by which completeness-claim is wanted. In particular, we can represent answers making the maximum completeness-claim in σ and S by

(45) $S \ \& \ Max(\sigma, S) \ \& \ D$, or $S \ \& \ Max(\sigma, S)$,

where $Max(\sigma, S)$ now needs defining.

Although the meaning of the maximum completeness-claim in σ and S is the same for whether- and which-questions, the problem of how to clothe the claim in notation $Max(\sigma, S)$ requires rather different treatments in the two cases. First, whether-questions. We are given a lexical subject (6) and a selection (31) sanctioned by that subject, and we know from section 1.21 that (31) can be so taken in exactly one way. Evidently a convenient way to say that all of the truths among $A_1, \ldots, A_n$ are included among $S_1, \ldots, S_p$, which is the maximum completeness-claim, is to say that all of the other A's, i.e., those not among the S's, are false. We therefore define $Max(\sigma, S)$, *the maximum completeness-claim in σ and S*, as

(46) $\bar{B}_1 \ \& \ldots \& \bar{B}_r$,

where $\{B_1, \ldots, B_r\}$ is the set of all members of the subject (6) which are not in the selection (31). Since this does not pick out $Max(\sigma, S)$ uniquely, we add some arbitrary stipulation for this purpose, say the requirement that $B_1, \ldots, B_r$ be a subsequence of (6). If all of the members of (6) happen to be in (31), so that the selection has already selected all of the presented alternatives, then since no further claim to completeness need be made, we let (46) be the empty symbol and suppose formulas in which it appears adjusted as to signs of conjunction.

Example: Suppose we put the complete-list question

(47)   *Which of lamb, beef, veal, and ham is on sale today?*

by means of a whether-interrogative $?\rho(L, B, V, H)$ with subject

(48) (L, B, V, H),

where the interpretation of the letters is the obvious one. Then $Max((48), L\&V)$ is $\bar{B}\&\bar{H}$, $Max((48), L)$ is $\bar{B}\&\bar{V}\&\bar{H}$, and $Max((48), L\&B\&V\&H)$ is the empty symbol.

Turning now to which-questions, let us suppose that the lexical subject σ is (17) and that the selection S, sanctioned by (17) is

(49) $Aa_{1_1} \ldots a_{1_n} \& \ldots \& Aa_{p_1} \ldots a_{p_n}.$

It will be recalled that completeness-claims for which-questions are to be construed in terms of real alternatives, so that we want $Max(\sigma, S)$ to say that each of the real alternatives presented by (17) that is true is signified, relative to (17), by some member of (49). So that we may see the intention through the notation, let us first define $(x_{1,n} = a_{k_{1,n}})$ as the conjunction $(x_1 = a_{k_1})\& \ldots \&(x_n = a_{k_n})$. Then for σ, a which-subject (17), and S a selection (49) sanctioned by (17), we define $Max(\sigma, S)$ as

(50) $\quad \forall x_1 \ldots \forall x_n [C_1 x_1 \& \ldots \& C_r x_r \supset [A x_1 \ldots x_n \supset$

$\quad\quad [(x_{1,n} = a_{1_{1,n}}) \lor \ldots \lor (x_{1,n} = a_{p_{1,n}})]]]$,

and call it the maximum completeness-claim in σ and S. It is a matter of tedious but elementary semantics to determine that $Max(\sigma, S)$ is true in an interpretation if and only if each of the true real alternatives in the real range of σ is signified, relative to σ, by some conjunct of S.

Example: Using "$P(x)$" for "x *is a prime between 10 and 20,*" the subject of the complete-list which-question (22) would have the form

(51) $\quad (x$ *is an integer* $// P(x))$.

Then $Max((51), P(11)\&P(13)\&P(17))$ would be

(52) $\quad \forall x [x$ *is an integer* $\supset [P(x) \supset [(x = 11) \lor (x = 13)$

$\quad\quad \lor (x = 17)]]]$,

and is the clause implied by the giving of (42) as a coded answer to (22).

The notion of a maximum completeness-claim in σ and S— $Max(\sigma, S)$—makes sense also when σ is abstract and X is abstract or nominal, and we suppose it defined in these cases, with some arbitrary convention securing uniqueness. It also makes a certain amount of sense when S is a real selection in an interpretation M, but since we are not in this case guided to any particular piece of notation, no comparable definition is possible.

B. In providing notation for completeness-claim specifications in interrogatives, about all we need to do is try to make it memorable. We shall use the dash, –, for the *lexical empty completeness-claim specification,* which is to go in place of *c* in (34) and (35), so that interrogatives not specifying a completeness-claim now look like

(53) $?(s - d)\sigma.$

We need worry besides only about the maximum completeness-claim specification. Since the abstract maximum completeness-claim specification is the universal quantifier, we shall use the sign of universal quantification, $\forall$, for the *lexical maximum completeness-claim specification,* which when put in place of *c* in (35) makes interrogatives specifying the maximum completeness-claim look like

(54) $?(s \ \forall \ d)\sigma.$

We shall say of (53) that it *specifies no completeness-claim,* and of (54) that it *specifies the maximum completeness-claim.*

C. the following definitions relate our notation for completeness-claims on the one hand and for completeness-claim specifications on the other.

First, for an interrogative *I* and a selection *S* sanctioned by *I,* we define *Comp(I, S)—the completeness-claim sanctioned by I relative to S*—in such a way that generalization to other completeness-claims besides the maximum will be straightforward, though we do not carry out such a generalization in this paper. If *I* specifies *no* completeness-claim, i.e., has the *empty* completeness-claim specification, then *Comp(I, S)* is undefined, while if *I* specifies the maximum completeness-claim, i.e., has the maximum completeness-claim specification, then *Comp(I, S)* is defined, of course, as *Max(σ, S)* where σ is the subject of I, Were we to have notations for completeness-claims other than just the maximum, one would expect $Comp(I, S)$ to take on other values accordingly.

Second, we may fill our definition of "direct answer," though it will still remain anticipatory and partial. For I an interrogative and A a formula, a necessary condition that A be a *direct answer* to I is that either I specifies no completeness-claim and A has, of the forms (30), one of the forms S or $S\&D$, where S is a selection sanctioned by I; or I specifies some completeness-claim (restricted here to be the maximum) and A, of the forms (30), has one of the forms $S\&Comp(I, S)$ or $S\&Comp(I, S)\&D$.

Examples: It is instructive to see how the concepts of selection-size specification and completeness-claim specification can be used to (incompletely) crossclassify questions. We present the matter in tabular form, awarding at the same time a name for each of the four resulting kinds of question and exhibiting the appropriate interrogative. Note that (51) is the common subject for each of the four.

Selection-size specification	Completeness-claim specification	
	Empty: –	Maximum: $\forall$
Single alternative $\begin{smallmatrix}1\\1\end{smallmatrix}$	*Single-example question* (27) $?(^1_1 - d)\,(51)$	*Unique alternative question* (26) $?(^1_1 \forall d)\,(51)$
Almost nonlimiting $\bar{1}$	*Some-examples question* (28) $?(^-_1 - d)\,(51)$	*Complete list question* (22) $?(^-_1 \forall d)\,(51)$

These type-names accrue to requests as well as questions. Indeed, the single-example question, for example, is such just because it "makes" the single-example request ($_1^1 - d$). What the table shows is that the selection-size and completeness-claim elements of a request can vary quite independently.

Single-example and some-examples questions sanction no completeness-claims, so that $Comp(?(_1^1 - d)$ (51), S) and $Comp(?(_1^- - d)$ (51), S) are undefined. On the other hand, $Comp(?(_1^1 \forall d)$ (51), $P(11)$) is $Max((51), P(11))$, i.e., $\forall x[x$ is an integer $\supset [P(x) \supset (x = 11)]]$. And $Comp(?(_1^- \forall d)$ (51), $P(11)\&P(13)\&P(17))$ is (52). We omit formal exemplification of many-place complete-list which-questions like (12).

There are whether-questions of each of the four varieties mentioned in the table above, though some are hard to put in English, a fault of English rather than our analysis. It is easy enough to find straightforward examples of questions specifying the maximum completeness-claim, especially the unique alternative variety, so much so that it is not surprising that some of the earlier erotetic logicians thought that every question was of the unique-alternative variety. But they were wrong. The following, which we take as whether-questions, are examples, respectively, of single-example, complete list, and unique alternative whether-questions.

(55)   *Which of the kitchen, the pantry and the wine cellar*
        seems to you as likely a place as any to commence
        looking for the missing hat pin?

(56)   *Was her ladyship wearing the emerald necklace, the*
        diamond bracelet, or both?

(57)   *Was it suicide or murder?*

Using obvious abbreviations, we would render these respectively in the forms $?(^1_1 - d)$ (K, P, W), $?(^-_1 \; \forall \; d)$ (E, D), and $?(^1_1 \; \forall \; d)$ (S, M).

Naturally, we do not insist that the questions must be taken as we suggest, only that they can be. Even so, it seems extremely difficult to put a some-examples whether-question unambiguously into English without using the "colon method" illustrated in the following:

(58)   *What's at least one example of a truth among the*
        following: the butler is concealing something, the
        upstairs maid knows more than she's telling, it would
        be worth questioning the gardener once again?

The interrogative for this would have the form $?(^-_1 - d)$ (B, M, G).

What about yes-no questions? With G for *Glass is a liquid at 70°F.*, should (2) be given as $?(^1_1 - d)$ $(G, \bar{G})$ or as $?(^1_1 \; \forall \; d)$ $(G, \bar{G})$? Since the interrogatives turn out to be answer-equivalent, and obviously so, not much hinges on the choice. From an information-processing point of view the former is somewhat preferable, since leading to answers which, because of not containing a completeness-claim, are shorter. One will prefer the latter if he thinks "yes" means *Glass is a liquid at 70°F., and it is false that glass is not a liquid at 70°F.*, where the completeness-claim, though redundant, is made explicit. Of course, there is no need to make a once-for-all decision, since one can treat some yes-no questions in one way and some in the other. Indeed, some may prefer to take some yes-no questions as $?(^-_1 \; \forall \; d)$ $(G, \bar{G})$ or as $?(^-_1 - d)$ $(G, \bar{G})$, which would allow the contradictory "yes and no" answer $G \,\&\, \bar{G}$. Since the inconsistency and consequent foolishness of this sentence would be so obvious to both questioner and respondent alike, no real damage would be likely to ensue from permitting it to count as a direct answer.

Some readers will wonder about the necessity of the completeness-claim specification: can it not be made part of the subject itself? Such problems are in certain contexts important, but not in ours, for we are designing a logic to be useful, which makes the question of the necessity of some linquistic feature beside the point. And the usefulness of the completeness-claim specification can hardly be doubted. Important or not, nowever, we answer the question. A. For each whether-question interrogative, there is an erotetically equivalent single-example whether-interrogative (See 3.4 for the concept of erotetic equivalence.) B. Unique alternative which-interrogatives are erotetically equivalent to certain single-example which-interrogatives. And C., no some-examples which-interrogative is erotetically equivalent to a complete-list which-interrogative such as, for (22), ?($\bar{}_1$ ∀ *d*) (*x is an integer* // *P(x)*).

1.33 Distinctness-claim and Distinctness-claim Specification   The answers to certain which-questions contain not only a selection and a completeness-claim, but also a "distinctness-claim." Consider

(59)   *Who were the denouncers of Cataline?*,

which is evidently a complete list question having the form

(60)   ?($\bar{}_1$ ∀ *d*) (*x is a person* // *x is a denouncer of Cataline*).

To this question we would normally count

(61)   *Cicero and Tully*

as coding a false answer, since it implicitly makes the false claim that the selected alternatives are distinct. Note that both the selection and the implied completeness-claim of (61) are true. It is only in respect of the implied distinctness-claim that (61) fails to attain perfect truth. For similar reasons we would tend to count

(62)   *2, 3, 5, 7, and VII*

as coding a false answer to

(63)   *What are at least five examples of primes?,*

which has the form

(64) $?(_5^- - \boldsymbol{d})$ (*x is an integer // x is a prime*),

where for this cooked-up example we let the category condition "*x is an integer*" determine as its nominal category the set comprising both Arabic and Roman numerals. The reason we would take (62) as false is that while there are nominally five examples selected, there are really only four: the nominal alternatives coded by "7" and "VII" signify the same real alternative. We call this third and last part of a direct answer its *distinctness-claim*, since it is a claim that each member of the nominal selection signifies a distinct member of the real selection. In the paradigm case of a one-place which-question, it may also be construed as a claim that the individuals picked out by distinct alternatives in the nominal selection are themselves distinct. The concept is wholly inapplicable to whether-questions, since these do not ask for answers picking out individuals.*

Just as to whether-questions there surely are direct answers

---

*As we remarked, the character of our erotetic logic is partly a function of the assertoric logic on which we build. If we had begun with an assertoric logic having modal capabilities, i.e., the power to express the concepts of logical necessity, possibility, and the like, either as connectives or as metalinguistic predicates, then it would make sense to interpret distinctness-claims for whether-questions as claims that none of the alternatives in the selection are necessarily equivalent.

making no completeness-claim, so there may well be direct
answers to which-questions making no distictness-claim. If so,
English examples do not offer us much guidance to their
discovery, for in the usual cases the problem of distinctness
simply does not arise, either because there is only a single
alternative in the nominal selection, so that it is trivially not
possible to violate distinctness by having two nominal alternatives signify the same real alternative, or else because the
pertinent nominal category contains no distinct names with a
common denotation, unlike our cooked-up example (64)
where we construed the nominal category determined by
"*x is an integer*" as comprising both Arabic and Roman numerals. If we had confined the category to one or the other,
oddities like (62) could not have occurred. But one must not
push this too far: often we use categories in which distinct
names have the same denotation, as lay astronomers use both
"the Morning Star," and "the Evening Star" as names for
Venus. This example warns us that sometimes, like the
Babylonians, we do not know that several of the names we
use denote the same entity, so that we can hardly protect
ourselves in every circumstance from violating distinctness.

Nevertheless, it is chiefly when we have in mind a sophisti-
cated and flexible artificial language that there arises the
question of whether there is a distinctness-claim or not. In
designing our formal erotetic apparatus, it might be better
either always to omit or always to insert the distinctness-
claim. The former would be formally easier while the latter
would undoubtedly permit a closer fit with English. We shall,
however, retain both possibilities, since we wish to maximize
flexibility and to avoid constraining users of our apparatus
where we cannot anticipate all their purposes. Therefore, we
shall have to have an element of the question's request, the

function of which is to specify whether or not a distinctness-claim is called for: the *distinctness-claim specification.* The two sorts we call the *empty* and the *nonempty* distinctness-claim specification, the former requiring that no distinctness-claim be made, the latter that the claim be made that the nominal selection contains no redundancies.

We suggested in section 1.32 the possibility of various completeness-claims short of the maximum, but the analogy seems irrelevant here: an answer either does or does not make a distinctness-claim, with no middle ground tenable. The point is not that measures of intermediate degrees of distinctness are not meaningful, but that they do not appear to have a systematic use in erotetic logic. For this reason, we allow only the empty and the nonempty distinctness-claim specifications.

Since, as we mentioned above, the question of distinctness does not ordinarily arise in English explicitly, the cross-classification of questions arising out of allowing the distinctness-claim specification to vary independently of the selection-size and completeness-claim specifications will not prove as illuminating as the table in section 1.32. For the sake of uniform terminology, however, we propose forming a designation for question types by adding or not adding the word "distinct," according as the distinctness-claim specification is nonempty or empty. Further, since the distinctness-claim is redundant in connection with any question employing the single-alternative selection-size specification, the only interesting additions to the table of section 1.32 will be the *complete-and-distinct list question* and the *some-distinct-examples question,* which require distinctness-claims. Absence of the modifier "distinct" will indicate that no distinctness claim is called for. The foregoing is to be taken in such a way that there is such a thing as a unique-and-distinct-alternative question and a single-distinct-example question. As is correctly suggested by their names, however, these are entirely superfluous additions to our erotetic apparatus.

We assume for formal convenience that whether-questions always have a distinctness-claim specification, but it is invariably the empty specification.

Notation: To reflect the concept of the distinctness-claim in our notation, we must A. describe notation by which answers can make distinctness-claims, B. provide notation for distinctness-claim specifications for interrogatives, and C. define the appropriate relations between the two sorts of notation.

A. Direct answers, we recall, are to have one of the forms

(30)   *S&C&D, S&C, S&D, S,*

where S is the selection, C the completeness-claim, and D the distinctness-claim. The immediate problem is to define appropriate notation to put in for D, the distinctness-claim. Since signification of real alternatives by nominal alternatives is relative to a subject, it is clear that a distinctness-claim will depend, like a completeness-claim, on a subject and a selection. Accordingly, answers making distinctness-claims can be represented in one of the forms

$$S \text{ \& } C \text{ \& } Dist(\sigma, S), \text{ or perhaps } S \text{ \& } Dist(\sigma, S),$$

where $Dist(\sigma, S)$—*the distinctness-claim in σ and S*—needs defining.

First, to say that the ith and j^{th} conjuncts of a selection (49) signify, relative to a subect (17), distinct real alternatives, one wants $(a_{i_1} \neq a_{j_1}) \vee \ldots \vee (a_{i_n} \neq a_{j_n})$, which we write as $V_{(1 \leqslant k \leqslant n)} (a_{i_k} \neq a_{j_k})$. Then to say that each of the conjuncts of (49) signifies, relative to (17), a distinct real alternative, is to affirm this for each distinct pair *i, j* between 1 and *p*. We may assume *i* smaller than *j*. Consequently, where σ is (17) and S is (49), we define $Dist(\sigma, S)$ as the following conjunction of disjunctions:

$$(65) \quad \&_{(1 \leqslant i < j \leqslant p)} V_{(1 \leqslant k \leqslant n)} (a_{i_k} \neq a_{j_k}).$$

Example: The selection coded by (61) is

(66)   *Cicero is a denouncer of Cataline & Tully is a denouncer of Cataline.*

Then where σ is the subject of (60), $Dist(\sigma, (66))$ is simply *Cicero $\neq$ Tully.* And $Dist((23), (43))$ is $(11 \neq 13) \& (11 \neq 17) \& (13 \neq 17)$.

Many-place examples are regrettably more complicated. Let S, taken as a selection sanctioned by (12), be $(b_1$ *is a brother of* $g_1) \& (b_2$ *is a brother of* $g_2) \& (b_3$ *is a brother of* $g_3)$. Then the distinctness-claim in the subject of (12) and S would be $[(b_1 \neq b_2) V (g_1 \neq g_2)] \& [(b_1 \neq b_3) V (g_1 \neq g_3)] \& [(b_2 \neq b_3) V (g_2 \neq g_3)]$.

B. In defining an appropriate notation for interrogatives, we need only make it memorable. We shall use the dash, –, as the *lexical empty distinctness-claim specification,* and the usual sign of distinctness, the sign, $\neq$, of denied identity, for the *lexical nonempty distinctness-claim specification.* These are to go in place of *d* in (36) and (37), so that interrogatives have one of the two forms

(67)   ?(*s c* –)σ

(68)   ?(*s c* $\neq$)σ,

the former with the empty and the latter with the nonempty distinctness-claim specification. There is, however, the following stipulation: if σ is a whether-subject, (68) is not well-formed. We say that (67) *specifies no distinctness-claim,* while (68) *specifies a distinctness-claim.*

C. for distinctness-claims, interrogative notation is related to answer notation as follows. First, for an interrogative I and a selection S sanctioned by I, if I specifies no distinctness-claim, $Dist(I, S)$—*the distinctness-claim sanctioned by I relative to S*—is undefined, while if I specifies a distinctness-claim, $Dist(I, S)$ is defined as the previously explained $Dist(\sigma, S)$, with σ the subject of I. Then we say that for a formula A to be a *direct answer* to I, a necessary condition is that either I specifies no distinctness-claim, and A has, of the forms (30), one of the forms S or $S\&C$, with S a selection sanctioned by I, or I specifies a distinctness-claim, and A has, of the forms (30), one of the forms $S\& Dist(I, S)$ or $S \& C \& Dist(I, S)$, with S as above.

Examples: (59) should be formalized as

(69) $?(^{-}_{1}\ \forall \neq)$ (x *is a person* $//$ x *is a denouncer of Cataline*),

unless one wished not to call for a distinctness-claim, in which case one would use the dash, –, in place of the sign $\neq$. The complete-and-distinct list question,

(70)   *What are the square roots of 1/4?*

could come out

(71) $?(^{-}_{1}\ \forall \neq)$ (x *is rational* $//$ $x^2 = 1/4$),

where the nominal category determined by "*x is rational*" is the set of all positive and negative fractions "+ n/m," "m" not zero. Then one of the true answers would be, "*The square roots of +1/4 are the distinct entities +1/2 and –1/2,*" or $((+1/2)^2 = 1/4 \ \& \ (-1/2)^2 = +1/4)) \ \& \ Max(\sigma, S) \ \& \ Dist(\sigma, S)$ where S is the selection indicated and σ is the subject of (71). In this case $Dist(\sigma, S)$ would of course be just $(+1/2 \neq -1/2)$. An answer false because of its false distinctness-claim alone would be "*The square roots of +1/4 are the distinct entities +1/2, +2/4, and –1/2,*" with selection

(72) $((+1/2)^2 = +1/4) \ \& \ ((+2/4)^2 = +1/4) \ \& \ ((-1/2)^2 = +1/4).$

The first and second conjuncts do not, as would be claimed by the appropriate $Dist(\sigma, (72))$, signify, relative to (71), distinct real alternatives, since $+1/2 = 32/4$.

In the case of an artificial question-answering capability, there might or might not be justification for expecting a warranted distinctness-claim. Thus, one might or might not store as part of the background information on the data base that "the Pittsburgh Pirates" and "the Los Angeles Dodgers" denote distinct entities, and one might or might not provide a capability for discerning that the Pirate–Dodger game on July 24, 1968, is the same as the Dodger–Pirate game on July 24, 1968; This is an important reason why whether or not answers make distinctness-claims should be left open.

1.34 Elementary Questions and Their Answers; Abbreviations and Codes The grammar of elementary questions has been all but completed in the preceding three sections; only the final definition of the question-answer relationship itself is pending. Since we are here undertaking to define this relationship only for what we have called "elementary questions," we make explicit our definition of an *elementary interrogative* as an expression having the form $?\rho\sigma$, where σ is subject to the

constraints of the *"**Notation**"* parts of 1.21 and 1.22, and
ρ is subject to those of 1.31, 1.32, and 1.33. Then where I is
any elementary interrogative and A is any formula, we say
that A *is a direct answer to I* if and only if I has one of the
forms on the left and A has the matching form on the right,
and where throughout S is a selection sanctioned by I in the
sense of 1.31, $Comp(I, S)$ is as defined in 1.32, and $Dist(I, S)$
is as in 1.33.

I	A
$?(s--)\sigma$	S
$?(s \, \forall \, -)\sigma$	$S \, \& \, Comp(I, S)$
$?(s - \neq)\sigma$	$S \, \& \, Dist(I, S)$
$?(s \, \forall \neq)\sigma$	$S \, \& \, Comp(I, S) \, \& \, Dist(I, S)$

It is obvious that our notation for interrogatives is satisfactory in the sense that one can tell effectively whether or
not a given piece of notation is an elementary interrogative
(*effectivity*) and, given that it is, what question it puts
(*univocity*). With respect to effectivity, the only relevant
feature of our scheme not immediately apparent is the requirement that the property of being a category condition is
effective (1.0), obviously required to make interrogativehood
effective.

The analogue for direct answers is almost* equally obvious:
for an arbitrary formula A and interrogative I, one can tell
effectively *whether* it is an answer to I (effectivity) and, if so,
how it answers I (univocity). That is, given that A is a direct
answer to I, one can mechanically and unambiguously recover

---

*It would be absolutely obvious did every direct answer have three conjuncts,
but as things stand, one has to check something like $A_1 \& A_2$ to see under which
of the first three cases it can fall, or $A_1 \& A_2 \& A_3$ against the first and fourth
cases. And one has to watch out for the cases in which $Comp(I, S)$ is to be taken
as the empty symbol, with signs of conjunction adjusted. But everything turns out
all right in the end.

from A a list of the alternatives it selects, whether or not it is making, relative to I, a completeness-claim, and whether or not it is making, relative to I, a distinctness-claim. All this is only "relative to I" since a formula which can be construed as answering one question in one way can be taken as answering a different question in some other way. For example, every formula can be taken as an affirmative answer to some yes-no question.

We attach considerable importance to the fact that our constructions satisfy not only the "Fundamental Criterion," as we sometimes call it, of effectivity for direct answers, but also the criterion of "erotetic univocity." Rather than even suggest a proof of this, we will just mention the out-of-the-way elements of our scheme most relevant to satisfying these criteria: effectivity of nominal ranges of category conditions (1.0), use of many-place conjunction (1.0), and prohibition of a conjunction of alternatives as an alternative (1.21).

A desire for certain kinds of completeness also guides our formalization: we wish our interrogatives to be able to put "every possible question." and for each question to be able to get "every possible answer." In a larger sense, we cannot possibly succeed, as Harrah (1969-b) demonstrates by way of a Cantorian diagonal argument, but we might hope to be able to ask and answer every elementary question.

With respect to which-subjects, one may well feel as a limitation that, although the choice of matrix in (16) is unlimited, the category apparatus one is allowed to use as a target for the category mapping g of (16) is incomplete in the sense that there are sets of names which one might like to use in defining presented alternatives but which cannot be used because there is no category condition with those sets as their nominal range. But a diagonal argument shows that such completeness is impossible: there are more sets of names than there are one-place conditions. We must therefore be satisfied with an established list of category conditions, relative to which our expressive powers are indeed complete.

As for requests, there are four limitations worthy of note. In the first place, although a selection-size of zero makes sense in the context of our analysis, we have not allowed selection-size specifications having the form $_0^u$. This is a straightforward incompleteness. It is easily reparable in the presence of a maximum completeness-claim specification, but otherwise, allowing it would require introducing some such artificiality as counting a standard tautology $p \lor \bar{p}$ as a selection of size zero. Or perhaps there is a more natural course which we have overlooked. In the second place, we do not allow a distinctness-claim, for reasons given in 1.33, to be called for by a whether-question; but that limitation is a natural outgrowth of limitations on the assertoric foundation on which we build. Thirdly, we allow only one sort of completeness-claim. One could not allow all sorts of completeness-claims—there are just too many—but one might wish more than the single one we give. We leave to others the overcoming of this limitation. Fourthly, it is possible that other kinds of specifications should be included in the request. For example, one might follow up the interesting suggestion of Kubinski (1966) that size-specifications be applied not directly to selections but rather to each queriable independently. And almost any addition to the assertoric logic on which we build is likely to suggest new sorts of specifications. See, for example, notes on pages 31 and 61.

Turning now to answers, we suppose ourselves given an interrogative *I,* and we wish to be sure we can answer it in every possible way. Of course, we have defined answerhood for *I,* and we could make short with this requirement by identifying "every possible way" with what we have antecedently defined as *I*'s direct answers. But there is more to be said, since it is the definitions themselves which need justifying. For intelligent discussion we need some kind of abstract intermediary between interrogatives and direct answers which could give us a measure of our completeness.

For whether-questions, there is hardly any alternative not equivalent to defining an *abstract answer* as an ordered pair $\langle I, \{A_1, \ldots, A_n\} \rangle$, where $\{A_1, \ldots, A_n\}$ is an abstract selection sanctioned by *I*. Such an abstract answer is said to be *true in M* if all the A_i are true in *M*, and if, furthermore, the completeness-claim, if any is called for by *I,* is also true in *M*. It is inconceivable that any "possible way of answering *I*" cannot be represented by such an abstract answer, so that completeness means: for each abstract answer *A,* there is a formula, A', such that (1) A' is a direct answer to *I,* and (2) *A* is true in *M* if and only if A' is true in *M*. Obviously we succeed in satisfying this easy criterion.

The problem is more complicated for which-questions, for which, as one might expect, the real vs nominal distinction is the one wanted. Two points about the definition we are about to give: In the first place, and this point applies equally to abstract answers to whether-questions, it is somewhat easier, though not absolutely essential, to make the interrogative itself a part of its abstract or real answers, though we thought it important not to do this for direct answers, which are to be used for purposes of communication and hence should be kept as simple as possible; Secondly, what amounts to the selection of a real answer will be reified as a sequence instead of as a set in order to give "real" content to the distinctness-claim instead of, as heretofore, explaining it as

pertaining to the relation between the nominal and real
selections. But, so as to avoid conflict with our previous use
of "real selection," we shall say "sequenced selection,"
leaving the modifier "real" to be understood.

So a *sequenced selection sanctioned by I in M* is a (possibly
transfinite) sequence* of real alternatives presented by *I* in
M, the cardinality of which falls within the extremes specified
by the selection-size specification of *I*. And a *real answer to I
in M* is an ordered pair, the first member of which is *I*, and
the second of which is a sequenced selection to *I* in *M*. Then,
where *S* is a sequenced selection sanctioned by *I* in *M*, the
real answer ⟨*I, S*⟩ is said to be *true in M* just in case A. every
member of *S* is true in *M*, B. if *I* specifies the maximum
completeness-claim, then every true real alternative presented
by *I* in *M* lies somewhere within *S*, and C. if *I* specifies a
distinctness-claim, then no real alternative occurs more than
once in *S*.

To proceed further we need to rely on "answer univocity"
to guarantee that there is defined a notion of "signifies," so
that if *A* is a direct answer to *I, A* signifies, in *M*, a unique
real answer to *I* in *M*. It is obvious how in our case this definition should go, and we omit details. It has the essential property that *A* is true in *M* if and only if so also is the real answer
it signifies in *M*. Then we can first define "*complete in M*" to
mean that every real answer to *I* in *M* is signified by some
direct answer to *I*, and "*complete*" to mean "complete in
every *M*." And we fall doubly short of completeness.

In the first place, if there is any entity in the domain of *M*
which is not denoted by some term, then

(73) $?(^{1}_{1} - -)(x \mathbin{/\!/} Fx)$

---

*Here "sequence" means "well-ordering."

has a real answer (saying that Fx is satisfied by the undenoted entity) without any direct answer which signifies it. And exactly the same sort of thing happens if any category condition Cx contains in its real range in M some entity not denoted by any name in its nominal category:

(74) $?(^1_1 - -) (Cx // Fx)$

will have a real answer signified by no direct answer. These limitations are no fault of our erotetic apparatus, being due simply to the fact that the domains of some interpretations contain more entities than there are names to go around. They cannot be overcome, but they can be escaped if one confines oneself to interpretations in which every entity has a name and in which every entity in the real range of a category condition is denoted by a name in the nominal range of that category condition. (For a detailed discussion, see Belnap 1963, sect. 7.5)

The second limitation arises from the finitude of conjunctions:

(75) $?(^-_1 - -) (x // Fx)$

will have real answers (those with an infinitely long sequenced selection) not signified by any direct answers, the selections of which are, of course, all finite in length. This limitation could be overcome by defining it away, simply by declaring that the meaning of the almost nonlimiting selection-size specification is that any finite selection is sanctioned, so that sequenced selections could not outrun nominal selections (Belnap 1963, p. 48). But though tempting, that move now seems to us an ad hoc one. There is an important sense in which someone who asks

(76)   *Which numbers are prime?*

can be said "really" to want an infinitely long list, though of course we cannot give him one. The only way to escape this limitation is to confine oneself to interpretations with finite domains.

We can, however, be sure that our apparatus is complete up to these two limitations: if A is a real answer to I in M, the sequenced selection of which is finite, and if A is also such that for each real alternative $\langle f, Ax_1 \ldots x_n \rangle$ in its sequenced selection, then $f(x_i)$ is denoted by some name. And, furthermore, if x_i is governed by a category condition Cx_i, then $f(x_i)$ is denoted by a name which lies within the nominal category determined by Cx_i. And that is as much as one can reasonably expect.

We conclude our discussion of elementary questions and their answers with a few words about abbreviations and codes. Our primitive notation has been chosen with one eye on readability and the other on the closest possible fit with our logical analysis. For example, since each request, abstractly conceived, contains three specifications, we make the lexical request have three positions. If the notation were to be used very much, however, it would be desirable to introduce some conventions which would allow shortening without loss of readability. On the side of the request, the following seem the most useful conventions:

1. Drop parentheses around the request:
   $?s\ c\ d\ \sigma$ for $?(s\ c\ d)\ \sigma$.

2. Omit dashes in any of the four cases in which they can occur:
   $?(s)\sigma$ for $?(s--)\ \sigma$,
   $?(s\ \forall)\ \sigma$ for $?(s\ \forall\ -)\ \sigma$,
   $?(s \neq)\ \sigma$ for $?(s - \neq)\ \sigma$, and
   $?(_v\ c\ d)\ \sigma$ for $?(_v^-\ c\ d)\ \sigma$.

3. Omit "1" as lower limit (since it is almost no limit at all):
  $?(^u\ \boldsymbol{c}\ \boldsymbol{d})\ \sigma$ for $?(^u_1\ \boldsymbol{c}\ \boldsymbol{d})\ \sigma$.

If we combine these three suggestions, which may be done without ambiguity, then, using "(. . .)" for an arbitrary subject, we arrive at the following happy notation for the six sorts of questions to which we have awarded names:

$?^1(\ldots)$	single-example question,
$?(\ldots)$	some-examples questions,
$?{\neq}(\ldots)$	some-distinct-examples question,
$?^1\forall(\ldots)$	unique-alternative question,
$?\forall(\ldots)$	complete-list question,
$?\forall{\neq}(\ldots)$	complete-and-distinct-list question.

We shall, in the sequel, have frequent recourse to these abbreviations, and only to these.

On the side of subjects, we can also let a formula A, standing alone without parentheses in the subject position of an interrogative, abbreviate certain most-commonly-used subjects related to A. Which subject A abbreviates we let depend on the variables occurring free therein. If A contains *no* free variables, then it is to be taken as standing for the yes-no subject $(A, \bar{A})$, while if A contains exactly the free variables $x_1, \ldots, x_n$ (given in some fixed order), then A stands for the category-free which-subject $(x_1, \ldots, x_n \ {/\!/}\ A)$. Then a yes-no question for closed A would be given by $?^1A$, or even $?A$ if one wished to call $A\&\bar{A}$ ("yes and no") a direct answer, even if a foolish one. And the category-free unique-alternative question about Fxy would be given by $?^1\forall Fxy$.

With respect to answers, the following codes seem workable. Note that these coded answers can be disambiguated only relative to some interrogative.

1. In this first place, relative to a given interrogative I having

the form ?$\rho\sigma$, an answer is fully determined by its selection,
S alone, since the completeness-claim and distinctness-claim,
when present, are always $Comp(I, S)$ and $Dist(I, S)$ respectively, and whether or not they are present is determined by
the interrogative I. Therefore, if S is a selection sanctioned by
I, we may define S as a *coded answer* to I, and as *code for*,
relative to I, its supplementation by whichever of $Comp(I, S)$
and $Dist(I, S)$ is called for by I.

2. This is as far as we can go on whether-questions, unless
we wish to do something like taking advantage of the ordering of the alternatives in a lexical whether-subject to refer to
alternatives by number, e.g., "1&3" for the selection $A\&C$
sanctioned by (A, B, C, D). But more is possible for which-
questions, since alternatives are fully determined by ordered
n-tuples of names just by plugging them into the matrix. And
a selection of size p is fully determined by a list of length p
of n-tuples of names. We may therefore take such a list, with
punctuation and English words where convenient, as a *coded
answer* to a which-interrogative, and as *code for*, relative to I,
the result of first determining the selection by substitution
into the matrix of I and then by supplementation with $Comp$
(I, S) and $Dist(I, S)$, as above.

Examples: Given (47) taken as ?$\forall(L, B, V, H)$, the sentence $L\&B$ would code $(L\&B)\&(\bar{V}\&\bar{H})$, just as in English
"*Lamb and beef*" codes "*Lamb and beef, but neither veal nor
ham.*"

If (12) is taken as ?$\forall\neq(x \text{ is a boy}, y \text{ is a girl} \;//\; x \text{ is a brother}$
of y), then *Jeff and Robin, Jeff and Wendy, Charlie and
Nancy, Chuck and Jody, and Matt and Sarah* is code for the
following, where quantifiers, horseshoes, and wedges are in
English: (*Jeff is a brother of Robin & Jeff is a brother of
Wendy & Charlie is a brother of Nancy & Chuck is a brother*

of Jody & Matt is a brother of Sarah) & (for all x and y, if x
is a girl & y is a boy, then if x is a brother of y, then either
x = Jeff & y = Robin, or x = Jeff & y = Wendy, or x = Charlie
& y = Nancy, or x = Chuck & y = Jody, or x = Matt & y =
Sarah) & (for all x and y, either Jeff ≠ Jeff or Robin ≠
Wendy, & either Jeff ≠ Charlie or Robin ≠ Nancy, & either
Jeff ≠ Chuck or Robin ≠ Jody, & either Jeff ≠ Matt or
Robin ≠ Sarah, & either Jeff ≠ Charlie or Wendy ≠ Nancy, &
either Jeff ≠ Chuck or Wendy ≠ Jody, & either Jeff ≠ Matt
or Wendy ≠ Sarah, & either Charlie ≠ Chuck or Nancy ≠
Jody, & either Charlie ≠ Matt or Nancy ≠ Sarah, & either
Chuck ≠ Matt or Jody ≠ Sarah).

2   The Grammar of Other Sorts of Questions

There are various sorts of questions other than the elementary which are amenable to the sort of analysis we have suggested. We discuss them briefly. The chief point in each case (except that of relativized questions in 2.4, which are a somewhat different matter) is to define an appropriate question-answer relationship.

2.1 Elementary-like Questions   The questions we discuss in this section might have been called "elementary" if our terminology had not hardened too early, since, like elementary questions, they have each a subject and a request and do not arise from any procedure of compounding.

There are in the first-order functional calculus as we have described it six fundamental parts of speech: open and closed formulas, open and closed-terms, truth-functional connectives, and quantifiers. Which-questions may be described as *positing* an open formula (matrix) and wanting closed terms (names) as *desiderata,* relying on the natural mode of combining an open formula with a name to form a sentence, i.e., substitution, to suggest the sort of alternative wanted. What we do here is to take the notions of posit and desiderata half seriously in order to see what happens if we let the posits be from any one of the six categories and the desiderata from any other. For instance, whether-questions may be described as positing a sequence of statements and wanting a truth-function thereof, where the natural mode of combination leading to the appropriate concept of *alternative* is the putting of the statements together in the manner specified by the truth-function. (This is not of course our standard way of looking at the matter. The idea is due to Stahl 1962.) We shall not try to make sense out of all thirty-six combinations, for we do not like to essay the impossible, and in any event we present what follows as an only partly baked idea.

This table, in addition to having which-question and whether-question entries, sums up the elementary-like questions we plan to discuss:

Posits   Desiderata

	Closed term	Open formula	Closed formula	Connective	Quantifier	Open term
Closed term	Identity-questions	Description-questions				
Open formula	Which-questions	What-questions			How-many-questions	
Closed formula				Whether-questions		
Connective						
Quantifier						
Open term						

Description-questions: As we remarked, which-questions posit open sentences (matrices) and want closed terms as their desiderata. Just opposed to these are the description-questions which posit a term and want in return open sentences, in this context called *descriptors*, as desiderata. The natural sentence-forming operation is again clearly substitution. For example,

(77)   *What color is Tom?*

posits "*Tom*" and wants a description, of a certain sort, of Tom. Alternatives presented by (77) have forms like *Tom is white, Tom is red,* etc., arising out of the substitution of the single posit "*Tom*" into each of the desiderata "*x is white*," "*x is red*," etc. Other examples would be "*What is Tom's occupation?*", "*How does your garden grow?*", and some senses of some who-questions such as "*Who was Scott?*"

In a second- or higher-order language having names for the properties which are expressed by descriptors, these questions might be taken as which-questions asking for the names of the properties applying to the denotation of the posited term. But nominalists insist that such questions should not be taken in such a way, and most of us can agree that they need not be so taken. In order to approach their formalization in a first order way, we need to suppose L equipped with a list of *determinables,* which are conditions with one free variable (we ignore many-place variants), with each of which is associated a list of *descriptors.* Thus, we would let the condition "*x is a color*" be a determinable, and its associated descriptors would be "*x is red*," "*x is puce*," etc. It would be natural to add to our definition of "interpretation" that a candidate interpretation *M* is an interpretation only if, in addition to previous requirements, an individual satisfies a determinable if and only if it satisfies some descriptor associated with that determinable.

Let *Hx* be a determinable. Then, to posit a term *b* and require a desiderata the descriptors $H_1 x, \ldots, H_i x, \ldots$, associated with *Hx,* one would use a new sort of subject,

(78)   *Des(Hx // b),*

and define its *range* as the set of presented alternatives $H_1 b$, $\ldots, H_i b, \ldots$.

> **Example:**   *What color is Tom?* would have as its subject

Des(*x is colored* // *Tom*) and present alternatives like "*Tom is red*," "*Tom is puce*," etc. How does this sort of subject combine with our various forms of request? Selection-size specifications certainly come through unscathed, and distinctness-claims can make perfectly good sense as well, since in the first order functional calculus we have a natural, if imperfect, concept of distinctness for descriptors: they are distinct if they do not apply to exactly the same things. For instance, if the selection is $H_3 b$ & $H_6 b$, then the appropriate distinctness-claim is $\overline{\forall x(H_3 x \equiv H_6 x)}$. The generalization of this to selections of arbitrary size is straightforward, and we leave it to the reader. Completeness-claims, however, give us a stickier problem. Although it makes perfectly good sense to ask if one has omitted any of the true presented alternatives from the selection, in general there will be no way to say this in the first-order functional calculus. The claim would involve variables ranging over properties, and hence move us up an ontological level. We could easily take care of the special case in which the set of descriptors associated with a given determinable is finite, since then the range will be finite and the completeness-claim can be expressed through a finite conjunction; details are easily reconstructable.

Example: Some who-questions can be taken as description-questions; for example, "*Who was Scott?*" receives some slight illumination by being construed as ? $\neq$ *Des*(*x was an individual of historical interest* // *Scott*), with alternatives such as "*Scott was an 18th century author*," "*Scott was Mme. Pompadour's secret paramour*," etc. Also some how-questions can be taken in this way: "*How does your garden grow?*" might be taken as ?[1] *Des*(*x grows* // *your garden*), where the determinable "*x grows*" has associated with it descriptors like "*x grows well,*" "*x grows quickly,*" "*x doesn't grow so well,*" etc. But, of course, "*How does your rose synthesize carbohydrates?*" is not like that.

Identity questions have closed terms as both posits and desiderata. The best examples are undoubtedly who-questions of a certain sort, for example, "*Who was the author of Waverly?*" As subjects we use *Ident*($Cx \parallel b$), where b is the posit and Cx is a category condition with which is associated a set of terms $a_1, \ldots, a_i, \ldots$, as before. The *natural* sentence-forming mode of combination of closed term and closed tem in a first-order functional calculus with identity is of course identity, so that, given a posited term b and some desiderata $a_1, \ldots, a_i, \ldots$, the natural set of alternatives is the set of identity statements $b = a_1$, $b = a_2$, etc.

Example: The subject of the Waverly question might be taken as *Ident*(x *is a human male* $\parallel$ *the author of Waverly*). All parts of the request make sense for such subjects, which is hardly surprising in view of the fact that all of their work can be done by ordinary which-subjects in which the identity is built into the matrix ($Cx \parallel b = x$), for instance, (x *is a human male* $\parallel$ *the author of Waverly* = x). We therefore need to say no more about them.

What-questions: Though the English word "what" is used in many ways indeed, by a "what-question" we somewhat arbitrarily decide to mean a question with matrices (instead of terms) as both posits and desiderata. Given a matrix Ax as posit and a descriptor (as we shall say) Bx as desideratum, there are four natural sentence-forming modes of combination. The most natural is perhaps equivalence, $\forall x(Ax \equiv Bx)$, but necessary condition of Ax, $\forall x(Ax \supset Bx)$, sufficient condition of Ax, $\forall x(Bx \supset Ax)$, and nonempty intersection of

Ax and Bx, $\exists\,x(Ax\&Bx)$, are almost on a par in point of naturalness. We therefore want what-questions asking after equivalents of, after necessary conditions for, after sufficient conditions of, and after nonempty intersects of a posited matrix Ax. Various combinations are also possible, but these we will leave to be secured by composition of the more elementary forms we now define. The first new sort of subject is $Equiv(Hx \mathbin{/\!/} Ax)$, where Ax is a matrix and Hx a determinable. Where the descriptors associated with Hx are $H_1 x$, . . . , $H_i x$, . . . , the presented alternatives are defined as $\forall x(Ax \equiv H_1 x)$, . . . , $\forall x(Ax \equiv H_i x)$, ... In an exactly similar way, $Nec(Hx \mathbin{/\!/} Ax)$ presents alternatives $\forall x(Ax \supset H_1 x)$, . . . , $\forall x(Ax \supset H_i x)$, . . . , $Suf(Hx \mathbin{/\!/} Ax)$ presents $\forall x(H_1 x \supset Ax)$, . . . , $\forall x(H_i x \supset Ax)$, . . . , and $Inter(Hx \mathbin{/\!/} Ax)$, presents $\exists x(H_1 x \,\&\, Ax)$, . . . , $\exists x(H_i x \,\&\, Ax)$.

With respect to how these fit together with requests, the story is the same as for description-questions: selection-size specification and distinctness-claims are easily handled, while completeness-claims are manageable only in the finite case. We will call the genus of the four sorts of question *whatquestions,* and award the species titles respectively *equivalence-questions*, *necessity-questions*, *sufficiency-questions*, and *intersection questions.*

Examples: *"What is a prime?"* is probably intended as an equivalence-question, though the appropriate determinable is hard to isolate. Perhaps the following will do: $?^1 Equiv(x$ is a *number $\mathbin{/\!/} x$ is a prime)*, where the determinable "*x* is a number" has associated with it a fixed list of number-theoretic descriptors. The question *"What sorts of things are mammals?"* is ambiguous, it seems to us, as to whether it is a necessity-question or a sufficiency-question. In the former case, alternatives would be like "*Mammals are vertebrates*," while in the latter they would be like "*Horses are mammals.*" But "*What sorts of things are black?*" is clearly a sufficiency-question, while "*What sorts of things are black things?*" is clearly an equivalence-question or necessity-question. "*What sorts of things can be prime?*" is an intersection-question, even if the "can" is taken seriously as a modal operator.

How-many questions, that is, questions asking "*How many?*", posit an open sentence or matrix and ask for quantifiers as desiderata. Thus, "*How many things are brown cows?*" can be construed as positing "*x is a brown cow*" and requiring as desiderata quantificational expressions like "some," "all," "none," "exactly seventeen," "at least a hundred," "at most six," etc. Naturally, the "etc." would have to be restricted to those quantifiers that could be expressed in the first-order functional calculus with identity. An appropriate subject form might be $Howmany(Fx)$, but more formal work needs doing before we can offer a well-grounded definition of "alternative" for this kind of subject. Also needing investigation are such two-posit how-many questions as "*How many cows are brown?*", taken as asking which relational quantifier obtains between "*x is a cow*" and "*x is brown*" (see Prior and Prior 1955).

2.2 Why-questions   Given the present machinery, it is tempting to reduce a why-question like "*Why is 'Grünbaum' spelled with an umlaut?*" to a metalinguistic which-question, "*What's an example of a sentence counting as an explanation of '"Grünbaum" is spelled with an umlaut'?*", but that is too easy and too unilluminating and also wrongly suggests that there is something essentially metalinguistic about why-questions. Even so, such a construction does bring to light one fact about why-questions: they ordinarily should be taken as single-example questions and not as unique-alternative questions, for as we all say, the same fact may have alternative and equally good explanations.

The most interesting work on why-questions, indeed, the only sensible work known to us, has been done by Bromberger (1966-b). The chief point of his work, insofar as we make use of it here, is that an answer to the sort of why-question he considers invariably makes reference to what he calls an "abnormic law," that is, a law having a form something like "No A's are B's, except C's or D's." (We are considerably oversimplifying.) Since the lawlike character of such a sentence cannot be caught in the wholly extensional first-order functional calculus, we can only approximate its intent by the extensional formula

(79) $\forall x(Ax \supset (Bx \equiv (Cx \lor Dx)))$,

which it implies. For this reason, we cannot blithely add a logic of this sort of why-question to what we now have, since it would not be properly supported by the underlying assertoric apparatus. Let us, however, add the blessedly temporary bastard form

(80) $x($No Ax are Bx except $C_1 x$, or . . . or $C_n x)$

to our assertoric grammar, giving it no semantics except that it is known to be properly stronger than, and hence imply, the extensional formula analogous to (79). (More formally: a candidate interpretation assigns a truth value to each sentence (80) as a whole; and a candidate interpretation is an interpretation only if it does not make (80) true and the analogue to (79) false.)

Then we ask "*Why is c a B?*" with a why-interrogative

(81) $?^1 Why(x \mathbin{/\!/} Bx, c)$

and define the answers as Ac & C_ic & x(No Ax are Bx except $C_1 x$ or . . . or $C_n x$). Note that in terms of 2.1 there are two posits: one an open sentence and one a name.

> **Example:** *"Why is 'Grünbaum' spelled with an umlaut?"* would be $?^1 Why(x \mathbin{/\!/} x$ *is spelled with an umlaut,* "Grün-baum"), and a true answer might be ("Grünbaum" *is an English word*) & ("Grünbaum" *is borrowed from German*) & x(No x *is an English word* are x *is spelled with an umlaut* except x *is borrowed from German* or x *is borrowed from some nonGerman language which uses umlauts*). Code for this would of course be just " 'Grünbaum' *is borrowed from German,*" the appropriate abnormic law being left to context. Note that every direct answer to (81) implies $Bc,$ just as answering the Grünbaum question implies that "Grünbaum" is in fact spelled with an umlaut.

Teller (1974) finds problems in Bromberger's analysis of why-questions. We avoid them by leaving (80) nonextensional, but also, of course, unanalyzed. By so much our version of Bromberger's suggested solution is, in a sense, incomplete. But after all, the problem of lawlikeness is, given a sensible division of labor, one for the assertoric logician. We have simply assumed a solution to that problem and gone on to construe Bromberger's proposal as giving a meaning to why-questions in a language having items like (80) as part of its assertoric equipment. And it will be allowed, first, that that is not nothing, and second, that it is about as much as an erotetic logician can be expected to do. Even so, there is quite evidently much more to the difficult topic of why-questions than this. We refer the reader to Bromberger (1966) for a start and request that he keep us posted on his attempts

to make clear—for this is the problem—what counts as an
answer to a why-question.

2.3 *Compound Questions*   Elementary questions can be com-
pounded sensibly in various ways, some of which we treat
here. In particular, we treat two modes of combination,
Boolean and logical, and four sorts of arguments for these
modes of combination: questions, subjects, requests, and
statements. We will, however, by no means try to ring every
possible change on these.

2.31 *Boolean Operations on Questions*   Because the result of
performing Boolean operations on recursive sets yields again
recursive sets, it is a priori plausible that such operations
should be usable to construct new questions out of old without violating the Fundamental Criterion of the effectivity of
the interrogative-answer relationship (see sect 1.34).

Consider: *"Have you ever been to Sweden, or have you
ever been to Germany?"* This might on occasion be taken as
being completely answered by any of four alternatives, S, $\bar{S}$,
G, $\bar{G}$, though on other occasions it might be taken as equivalent to *"Have you ever been to Sweden, and have you ever
been to Germany?"* treated in section 2.32 below. In the
former case, we can either think of it directly as a single
elementary whether-question with four alternatives, or as a
compound question composed of two whether-questions by
the operation of union. To handle the latter concept, the
following notation seems simplest: If $I_1, \ldots, I_n$ are interrogatives, then $I_1 \cup \ldots \cup I_n$ is said to be a *unionized interrogative* and to be the *union* of all the I_i. For such an interrogative,
the concepts of subject, request, etc., are not defined at all,
but only the cardinal concept of direct answer: A is a direct

answer to $I_1 \cup \ldots \cup I_n$ if and only if A is a direct answer to at least one of I_i, which is to say that "the set of answers to the union of a series of questions" is "the union of the sets of answers to those questions." Then the Sweden–Germany question, in order to have S, $\bar{S}$, G, and $\bar{G}$ defined as its answers, could be asked by $?^1 (S, \bar{S}) \cup ?^1 (G, \bar{G})$.

Of course, $I_1 \cup I_2$ is not really the Boolean union of I_1 and I_2 since I_1 and I_2 are questions, and questions are not sets. But application of the concept still makes sense, since the most important feature of a question is the set of its direct answers, and as we have said, the set of the answers to the resultant question is indeed the Boolean union of the sets of direct answers to the ingredient questions. Generally speaking, whenever we refer to the application of a Boolean operation to questions, we intend that, as in the case of union, the set of answers to the new question be the result of applying the Boolean operation to the sets of answers to old questions.

Intersection of questions is as meaningful as union, although, we suspect, considerably less useful. It could be used in order to ask something like "*Tell me something which directly answers both I_1 and I_2,*" but we cannot think of any interesting examples. The sheer complementation of questions is like intersection in being meaningful but probably uninteresting, answering to locutions like "*Tell me anything that does not directly answer I.*" Of somewhat more use would be the Boolean operation of set difference: $I_1 - I_2$ could be used for "*Tell me something which answers I_1 without answering I_2;*" for instance, "*Tell me what life is like up at the front without telling me about the military situation.*" In the case of all Boolean operations on questions, it would be simplest to use the usual Boolean signs themselves between interrogatives, and, of course, the set of direct answers to the resultant interrogative is to be defined as the result of applying the Boolean operation whose sign stands between the interrogatives to the sets of direct answers of the interrogatives occupying argument positions. It is to be noted that for these sorts of interrogatives the concepts of subject and request are inapplicable, there remaining only the crucial concept of direct answer.

2.32 **Logical Operations on Questions** In the previous section we made new sets of answers out of old sets of answers by way of Boolean operations, but we did not create any new answers out of old. Now we do. The obvious way to make a new answer out of some old ones is by way of one of the standard logical operations. We are thus led to mean by "the result of performing a logical operation on a pair of questions," a new question, the answers to which are formed by performing the given logical operation on the answers to the ingredient questions.

Neither the negation of questions nor the disjunction of questions so conceived, much less the implication or equivalence of questions, seems of much interest, so we use conjunction of questions as our sole example. We define $I_1 \& \ldots \& I_n$ as the conjunction of interrogatives $I_1, \ldots, I_n$, and define its answers as conjunctions $A_1 \& \ldots \& A_n$, with A_i a direct answer to I_i. (Compare Harrah 1961.) The set of answers to a conjunctive interrogative can be conveniently visualized as a sort of Cartesian product of answers to its conjuncts.

Example: $?^1(S, \bar{S}) \& ?^1(G, \bar{G})$ would ask the second version of the Sweden–Germany question of 2.31 and would have as answers $S\&G$, $S\&\bar{G}$, $\bar{S}\&G$, and $\bar{S}\&\bar{G}$.

Probably the best thing to mean by "the decomposition of a question into a family of (simpler) questions" is something specifiable via the conjunction of interrogatives together with the semantic concept of the equivalence of interrogatives (see sect. 3.4). For example, it is *not* the case that yes-no questions are "fundamental" in the sense that every whether-interrogative I is equivalent to a conjunction $I_1 \& \ldots \& I_n$ of yes-no interrogatives.

The logical operation of conjunction of interrogatives can be expressed in English by "and," as in *"Where is Timbuctu and what is its population?"*, but the reason we call the operation "conjunction" is not this at all. It is rather entirely due to the fact that answers to the resultant interrogative are conjunctions of answers to the ingredient interrogatives. Here as elsewhere, it is the answers which count! To bring home this point, note that English "or" can also be used between interrogatives, as in *"How can one get from here to Detroit by plane, or how can one get there by automobile?"* But the logical operation of disjunction is not used in forming answers to the resultant interrogative (*"Either TWA has a flight leaving at 9:00 a.m. or Route 26 runs from here to there"* is no answer); instead the operation is union.

We can now see why the English locutions "and" and "or" do not preserve the duality relationship which the analogy with assertoric logic would suggest. In their erotetic use, between interrogatives, "and" tends to stand for a logical operation and "or" for a Boolean operation. The reason for this disparity of tendencies is that, as reflection shows, on the "and" side the logical operation of conjunction is interesting, but the Boolean operation of intersection is not, while on the "or" side the Boolean operation of union is entertaining, but the logical operation of disjunction is a bore. This in turn is related in ways we cannot now pursue to the fact that "*Either tell me that A or tell me that B* is not equivalent to "Tell me that *either A or B*," while "*Both tell me that A and tell me that B*" is equivalent to "Tell me that *both A and B*."

Naturally, not every "and" and "or" standing between English interrogatives is to be taken in the way we suggest. For example, "*Who or what killed the dog?*" seems to be "exclusive," in the sense that answering one of the ingredient interrogatives commits one to denying the presupposition of the other, so that where P_1 is the presupposition of I_1 and P_2 of I_2, the formal pattern would be something like $(\overline{P_2}/\&/I_1)$ $\cup(\overline{P_1}/\&/I_2)$, where $/\&/$ as between a statement and an interrogative is explained below in section 2.34. And "*Have you ever been to Sweden, or have you ever been to Germany?*" might be taken in still a third way as "inclusive," in the sense that one is permitted to answer either or both ingredient interrogatives, so that the formal analogue would look like $I_1 \cup I_2 \cup (I_1 \& I_2)$. Again, Stahl (1962) points out that sometimes "or" is not even symmetrical. For example, "*What day have you decided upon, or what week?*" suggests the form $I_1 \cup (\overline{P_1}/\&/I_2)$ and is thus a "corrections-accumulating question sequence" in the sense of Åqvist (1969) and Belnap (1969-a), *q.v.* Stahl's own example, "*Does Meier know the South Seas, or who here does know them?*", must be treated still differently, since the way the answers to the first ingredient question enter into the compound is not symmetrical. And "*Is it a bird or is it a plane?*" is not at all—contrary to appearances—the result of compounding the questions put by the ingredient interrogatives, but is just a way of asking the simple whether-question as to whether it is a bird on the one hand or a plane on the other. That is, the resultant question has just two answers, "*bird*" and "*plane.*" (We take "neither" as a correction.)

2.33 Operations on Subjects and Requests   Sometimes one can obtain a desired erotetic effect only by performing an operation on subjects instead of on questions. We shall illustrate by means of the union of subjects.

We begin with the appropriate definition: if $\sigma_1, \ldots, \sigma_n$ is a list of whether-subjects and which-subjects, then $(\sigma_1 \cup \ldots \cup \sigma_n)$ is a *unionized subject* and is the *union* of $\sigma_1, \ldots, \sigma_n$. Presented alternatives, including real and nominal ones, are defined simply as the Boolean union of alternatives presented by the various ingredient elementary subjects. And S is a selection sanctioned by such a subject if, exactly as before, it is a conjunction of alternatives presented by that subject.

Thus, let $\sigma_1 = (A, B, C)$ and $\sigma_2 = (D, E)$. Then the set of *alternatives presented by* $\sigma_1 \cup \sigma_2$ is just the union $\{A, B, C, D, E\}$ of those presented by σ_1 and σ_2. But what makes things interesting is that the set of *selections sanctioned by* $\sigma_1 \cup \sigma_2$ is not the union of those sanctioned by σ_1 and σ_2, since it includes selections like $A \& D$ sanctioned by neither. For this reason $A \& D$ will be an answer to $?_2^2((A, B, C) \cup (D, E))$ but not to $?_2^2(A, B, C) \cup ?_2^2(D, E)$. And, in general, the only case in which $?\rho\sigma_1 \cup ?\rho\sigma_2$ has the same answers as $?\rho(\sigma_1 \cup \sigma_2)$ is the case in which ρ is the single-example request $\binom{1}{1}--)$.

Definition of $Max(\sigma, S)$ requires some footwork for unionized subjects, though the underlying idea is simple enough: just find a way to say that every alternative presented by σ, but not signified by a conjunct of S, is false. We first define an auxiliary function, $Max^*(\sigma, S)$, having the feature that, unlike Max, it is defined for arbitrary S, whether or not S is sanctioned by σ. *Max** is first defined for elementary subjects. If no conjunct of S (including S itself) is in the range of σ, then *Max**(σ, S) is $\overline{A_1}$& . . . &$\overline{A_n}$ or $\forall x_1$ . . . $\forall x_n (C_1 x_1$ & . . . &$C_r x_r \cup \overline{Ax_1 . . . x_n})$, according as σ is (6) or (17). Otherwise, that is, if some conjunct of S is in the range of σ, let S_1' & . . . &S_r' be a conjunction, in order, of all the conjuncts of S which are in the range of σ, and then define *Max**(σ, S) as the previously defined *Max*$(\sigma, S_1'$ & . . . &$S_r')$. Then if σ is a unionized subject $(\sigma_1 \cup . . . \cup \sigma_n)$, we define *Max**$(\sigma, S)$ as *Max**(σ_1, S)& . . . &*Max**(σ_n, S) and, provided S is a selection sanctioned by σ, we can now define *Max*(σ, S) to be exactly *Max**(σ, S). Then *Comp*(I, S) is defined as before, and nothing more is to be said.

The meaning of the distinctness-claim for unionized subjects is to be that every real alternative signified, relative to any ingredient which-subject, is to be distinct from any real alternative signified relative to that same which-subject. So, first, let $\sigma_1', . . . , \sigma_r'$ be all the ingredient which-subjects in σ presenting at least one alternative in S, and for $1 \leqslant i \leqslant r$, define S_i' as a conjunction of all the conjuncts in S presented by σ_i'. Then simply define *Dist*(σ, S) as *Dist*(σ_1', S_1') & . . . & *Dist*(σ_r', S_r'), and proceed as before. In this way, all our concepts are sensibly generalized to unionized subjects.

Example: One of the most important reasons for wanting to go beyond elementary subjects such as (6) and (17) is to be able to ask *mixed which-whether questions* such as the following, which appears on the application form for a United States Passport:

(82)　　*I have never been married.* ____
　　　　I was first married on ____.

Evidently this question presents an infinity of alternatives, one explicitly the rest via a which-subject. Given union of subjects, (82) can be put by ?$^1\forall((I$ *have never been married*) $\cup$ (*x is a date* // *I was first married on x*)). Direct answers would have one of the forms "*I have never been married & there is no date on which I was first married*" or "*I was first married on x & it is not the case that I have never been married & x is the only date on which I was first married,*" where in each case the first conjunct is the selection and the others are parts of the completeness-claim. Of course, in this example the completeness-claim is redundant, exactly as it is for a yes-no question, but that would by no means be true in a more general case of a unique-alternative mixed which-whether interrogative ?$^1\forall((A_1, \ldots, A_n)\cup(x$ // *Fx*)). And note how different the effect of such an interrogative is from that of a union, ?$^1\forall(A_1, \ldots, A_n) \cup$?^{1} $\forall(x$ // *Fx*), of a unique-alternative whether-interrogative with a unique-alternative which-interrogative.

We omit discussion of compound subjects corresponding to other Boolean operations or to logical operations. In each case the decision as to whether one wants to apply the operation to subjects or to whole questions depends on the stage at which one wants the specifications contained in the request— especially selection-size specification and completeness-claim specification—to take effect. We also pass over the more complicated analysis of "abstract subject" which would be required to legitimate our constructions.

One could get the effect of the following question by using a "unionized request"

(83)   *If there are no more than five pairs of twin primes, which are they, or if there are more than five such, what are at least six examples?,*

for one wants a completeness-claim if the selection is of size
five or less, but no completeness-claim if it is larger. Let us
therefore say that if $\rho_1, \ldots, \rho_n$ are elementary requests,
then $(\rho_1 \cup \ldots \cup \rho_n)$ is a *unionized request,* and let us understand $?(\rho_1 \cup \ldots \cup \rho_n)\sigma$ exactly as the union, as explained in
section 2.31 above, of $?\rho_1 \sigma, \ldots, ?\rho_n \sigma$. (As we have seen,
unionized subjects cannot be treated in this way.)

Example: The twin primes question (83) could be given as
$?((^5_1 \forall \neq)\cup(^-_6 - \neq))\,(x,\,y\,//\,x\text{ and }y\text{ are primes, and }x{+}2 = y)$.
It would have as answers those formulas which are answers to
either $?(^5_1 \forall \neq)\,(x,\,y\,//\,x\text{ and }y\text{ are primes, and }x{+}2 = y)$ or
to $?(^-_6 - \neq)\,(x,\,y\,//\,x\text{ and }y\text{ are primes, and }x{+}2 = y)$. We
omit discussion of other Boolean operations on requests.

2.34 Logical Operations on Questions and Statements Prior and
Prior (1955) and others have pointed out the enormous differences between *hypothetical questions* such as

(84)   *If you were to go, would you take an umbrella?*

and *conditional questions* such as

(85)   *If you are going, are you taking an umbrella?*

The same contrast obtains between the hypothetical question,

(86)   *If you had a million dollars, on what would you be
        spending it?*

and the conditional question,

(87)   *If you have a million dollars, on what are you spend-
        ing it?*

  Since conditional questions require entirely new concepts,

we leave them for separate discussion (sect. 2.4), but hypothetical questions can be conceived as arising from a logical operation performed on a statement and (the answers to) a question.

The "if" in hypothetical questions occurs in the very direct answers called for, so that for instance the direct answers to (84) are *Yes: If I were to go, I would take an umbrella,* and *No: If I were to go, I would not take an umbrella.* Similarly, the direct answers to (86) are something like *If I had a million dollars, I would spend it on x, y, and z, and on nothing else.* The subjunctive is not essential to putting a hypothetical question in English; future tensed conditions will often do as well:

(88)   *If you acquire a million dollars, on what will you spend it?*

might well be taken as a hypothetical with direct answers *If I acquire a million dollars, I will spend it on x, y, and z, and on nothing else.* But in either event, the "material implication" of our formal language L is doubtless inadequate to the sense of "if" required.* Putting this aside, however, we can usefully increase our stock of interrogative forms by defining $(P /\supset/ I)$ as a hypothetical interrogative whenever P is a formula and I is an interrogative, defining the direct answers to $(P /\supset/ I)$ as the formulas $P\supset A$, where A is a direct answer to I. On this reading, to answer a hypothetical question is to answer the categorical part of it under a hypothesis or con-

---

*One of us has done some work on a concept of "relevant implication," which may be of some use here (Anderson and Belnap 1975, especially chapter five). Quite apart from this, there has been a good deal of recent research on subjunctive conditionals, largely accessible through R. Wolf's complete bibliography of entailment-related literature, to appear in volume II of *Entailment* (by A. R. Anderson, N. D. Belnap, Jr., and R. K. Meyer, Princeton University Press, forthcoming).

dition. This is all that erotetic logic can or should do for hypothetical questions; the problem of finding a better connective than ⊃ to adequately catch the required sense of "if" belongs to assertoric logic.

It is to be noted that we do not, for this sort of question, mediate the notion of "direct answer" by way of subject and request. The reason for this is twofold. In the first place, the concept of a hypothetical question makes sense where the question asked under the hypothesis is of any imaginable sort at all, irrespective of whether the concepts of subject and request are or are not applicable to it, just as long as it has "direct answerhood" defined for it—and every usable interrogative must satisfy this minimal condition. Second, if one attempted to derive a concept of "presented alternative" for hypothetical questions in the natural way by tacking the condition P onto the presented alternatives of I (if defined), the natural way of applying the apparatus of completeness-claims would give nonintuitive results. For example, *If today were Tuesday, which of beef or lamb would be on sale?* does not ask for a complete list of the truths among $P \supset B$ and $P \supset L$, together with a claim that the rest are false, so that answers would be like $(P \supset B)\&(\overline{P \supset L})$, but rather asks that a claim be made under the condition P as to a complete list of truths among B and L, so that answers are like $P \supset (B\&\overline{L})$. This is extremely important if the "if" is taken as material implication, since $(\overline{P \supset L})$ logically implies the truth of P. But it is also pertinent for other senses of "if."

Nevertheless, for some stronger senses of "if" it may turn out to be useful to form alternatives by way of a logical operation on the statement P and a subject, yielding a new subject. Then P would naturally appear as part of the resultant subject rather than as a qualification on the interrogative as a whole. The appropriate notation would be something like

$?\rho(P /\supset/ \sigma)$, where the range of the subject $(P /\supset/ \sigma)$ is taken
as the set of formulas $P \supset A$, with A an alternative in the
range of σ. Direct answers would be defined in the usual way
via the request and subject.

An erotetic form closely related to hypotheticals is the
"given that" question, as for example,

(89)   *Given that you are going, are you taking an umbrella?*

with answers *Yes: I am going, and taking an umbrella.* and
No: I am going, but not taking an umbrella. The idea is that
answering a "given that" question in any way at all commits
one to affirming the "given that" clause, which hence may be
thought of as appearing in each direct answer. The most
honest way of asking (8) is doubtless as a given-that question:

(90)   *Given that John used to beat his present wife, has he
         a wife whom he used to beat and has now stopped
         beating?*

Since a given-that question arises out of conjoining a statement with a direct answer, we suggest the notation $(P /\&/ I)$,
where P is a formula and I is an interrogative. Then we define
the direct answers to $(P /\&/ I)$ as the result of conjoining P to
the direct answers to I. Thus, if I is $(U /\&/ ?^1(S, \bar{S}))$, where U
is "*John used to beat his wife,*" it will have as answers the
two formulas $U\&S$ and $U\&\bar{S}$. It is therefore obviously equivalent to $?^1(U\&S, U\&\bar{S})$, though the former interrogative is
more transparent with respect to its form.

We might have called "hypothetical questions" by the name
"added-condition questions" since their answers are generated
by uniformly adding a condition to a given set of direct answers. On similar gounds, given-that questions might have
been called "added-conjunct questions." We leave it to the

reader to determine whether or not there is any point in
introducing "added-disjunction," or "added-equivalence"
questions, though we prefer to leave him no option with
respect to "added-Sheffer-stroke questions."

2.35 Quantification into Questions   One can hardly avoid con-
sidering the notations $\forall xI$ and $\exists xI$, where x is free in I
(hence not a queriable of I), and wondering what they are
good for. If $I_1 \& \ldots \& I_n$ means "Answer every I_i," then
presumably $\forall xI$ should mean "Answer I for every entity x
in the domain." This sounds like an infinite task, except, of
course, in finite domains or to the extent that we have a
finite way of answering I for infinitely many x. As an ex-
ample of the latter, given $\forall x ?^1 (Px, \overline{Px})$, ("*For each x, is x a
P or not?*"), the formula $\overline{Pa} \& \overline{Pb} \& \overline{Pc} \& \forall x(x \neq a \& x \neq b \&$
$x \neq c \supset Px)$ (i.e., "*a, b,* and *c* are not P's, but everything else
is") seems to answer $?^1 (Px, \overline{Px})$ for every x, and to do it
finitely. We generalize upon this idea as follows. Let I be an
interrogative, with x free; then we define the direct answers
to $\forall xIx$ as conjunctions $A_1 a_1 \& \ldots \& A_n a_n \& \forall x(x \neq a_1 \& \ldots$
$\& x \neq a_n \supset Bx)$, where $A_1 x, \ldots, A_n x$, and Bx are all direct
answers to I. One observes that every answer to $?^-_1 \forall (x // Px)$
is a notational variant of an answer to $\forall x ?^1 (Px, \overline{Px})$, but not
conversely.

    In order to obtain the effect of categoreally qualified ques-
tions such as "For each x which is a C, is x a P or not?" we
need some notation restricting the range of the quantifier to
a category. Where Cx is a category condition, we use $\forall_{[Cx]} I$.
Its direct answers are defined as $A_1 a_1 \& \ldots A_n a_n \& \forall x(Cx \supset$
$(x \neq a_1 \& \ldots \& x \neq a_n \supset Bx))$, where $A_1 x, \ldots, A_n x$, and Bx
are all direct answers to I as above, and where furthermore
each a_i is in the nominal category determined by Cx. Then

$\forall_{[Cx]} ?^1 (Px, \sim Px)$ bears the same relation to $?^-_1 \forall (Cx \mathbin{/\!/} Px)$ as $\forall x ?^1 (Px, \sim Px)$ does to $?^-_1 \forall (x \mathbin{/\!/} Px)$.

Another case in which a universal quantification into an interrogative could be finitely answered arises when the range of the variable of quantification is limited to a finite category. To allow for this, we would need in our assertoric logic a grammatically given list of *finite category conditions* and an effective way of determining for each the number of names in its nominal range. The list could include those conditions having the form $x = a_1 \vee \ldots \vee x = a_n$, and we would need so to define the semantic notion of interpretation that to be such, a candidate interpretation must put nothing in the real range of a finite category condition which is not denoted by some name in the nominal range of that condition. Then where Cx is one of our finite category conditions, we could define the answers to $\forall_{[Cx]} I$ as conjunctions $A_1 a_1 \& \ldots A_n a_n$, where the a_i run through the n names in the nominal range of Cx, and where, as before, $A_1 x, \ldots, A_n x$ are direct answers to I. Thus, if "$10 < x < 20$" were one of our finite category conditions and had the nominal range $\{11, \ldots, 19\}$, and where Px ix "x *is prime*," $\forall_{[10<x<20]} ?^1 (Px, \overline{Px})$ would be a way of asking (22).

With respect to $\exists x I$, we have not found a use for it and do not expect to unless we can first find employment for the finite logical operation of disjunction on interrogatives, of which it would be a generalization. In contrast, a quantificational generalization of union should be useful. Given $\cup x I$ with x free in I, we define its direct answers as Aa, where Ax is a direct answer to Ix. Hence, $\cup x I$ corresponds to the locution, "Answer me I for some x in the domain." Note that $\cup x ?^1 (Px)$ has exactly the same answers as $?^1 (x \mathbin{/\!/} Px)$. We mention in passing that categoreal qualification is also applicable to $\cup x I$.

We leave for another occasion development of the conceptual analysis, including analysis of being an "answer to *I* for the entity *x*," which is required to support the legitimacy of these interrogative forms. For other approaches to quantification, see Åqvist (1965), Woods (1968), and Hintikka (1974).

2.4   Relativized Questions; Conditional Questions   We turn now to the problem of conditional questions raised in section 2.34, which will lead us to the more general concept of "relativized" questions.* We begin with the observation that the difference between (85) and (87) on the one hand and the hypotheticals (84) and (86) on the other is that the former, unlike the latter, do not call for answers having the form of a conditional (i.e., "if . . . "), but rather ask that an answer, itself unconditional in form, be supplied only if a certain condition is true. The intent of (85), as we read it, is that an answer is called for only if the respondent is going; if he is not going, then although he may take it upon himself to so inform the questioner, to do so is not directly called for.

One difficulty in generalizing from such examples is that English has no short and idiomatic interrogative way of making the distinction we require, since, as it seems to us, (85) could be taken as a plain hypothetical $(G /\supset/ ?^1 (U, \sim U))$, or even as an elementary whether-question $?^1 (\sim G, U, \sim U)$, with the negation of the condition as an additional direct answer. More unambiguous would be the following, which we take to be an equivalent of (85): *"If you are going, tell me whether you are taking your umbrella."* Further, it is by no means clear to us that at the level of abstraction at which we are operating there is an enormous amount of utility in conditional questions, but since they will likely come into their own once parameters governing the time and other aspects of

*See also Belnap 1972 and references therein.

the erotetic situation are introduced, since they allow a substantial deepening of our understanding of certain aspects of erotetic logic, and since they have never before been given an entirely satisfactory treatment, we append a few words about them.

The most important remark we have to make about an interrogative putting a conditional question is that it is a horse of a different hue, since its characterization requires brand-new fundamental metalinguistic concepts. For the interrogatives we have treated to date, the fundamental metalinguistic locution has invariably been "*A* is a direct answer to *I*," with *A* a formula and *I* an interrogative. But even to begin discussion of interrogatives which sometimes call for answers (if a condition is true) and sometimes do not call for answers (if a condition is false) requires a different fundamental metalinguistic locution. Guided not only by conditional questions, which like yes-no questions are misleading in their simplicity, but also by some other types, we are led to the following pair of fundamental locutions, where *I* is an interrogative, *M* is an interpretation, and *A* is a formula: *I calls for an answer in M* and *A is a direct answer to I in M.* It is understood that the second locution is only defined provided that *I* calls for an answer in *M*. We will use *is operative* as a synonym for "calls for an answer," and say that an interrogative is *inoperative* if it does not call for an answer.

Interrogatives for which only the unrelativized-to-*M* locution "*A* is a direct answer to *I*" is defined are *absolute,* while a *relativized* interrogative is one for which direct answerhood is relativized to interpretations. In order to understand what question is put by an absolute interrogative, we said it was necessary to know what counts as a direct answer. Just so, to understand what question is put by a relativized

interrogative it is necessary to know A. in which interpretations it calls for an answer, and B. for those interpretations M
in which it calls for an answer, what its direct answers are in
M.

In order to subsume an absolute interrogative I under the
new concepts, we will say that the new locutions apply to it
in the following ways: A. I calls for an answer in *every M,* and
B. its direct answers in every M are the same, namely, those
previously defined as its direct answers in the absolute sense.

The distinction between "absolute" and "relativized" interrogatives depends on which metalinguistic locutions are
appropriate. Among the relativized interrogatives, however,
we can single out those as *categorical* which A. call for an
answer in every M and B. have the same direct answers in
every M. When absolute questions are relativized as above
they obviously turn out to be categorical, but, of course,
there are other sorts of categorical relativized questions.

Conditional interrogatives, however, are clearly not all
categorical, since they do *not* always call for an answer. Let
us agree to use $(P \mid I)$ as the *conditional interrogative* with
condition P and *conditioned* interrogative *I.* But what does
this notation mean? It follows from the above that to say
what question this interrogative puts we must say A. in which
interpretations M it calls for an answer, and B. for those in
which it so calls, what its direct answers are. Application of
these ideas is straightforward: $(P \mid I)$ *calls for an answer in M*
iff P is true in M and I calls for an answer in M; provided
$(P \mid I)$ calls for an answer in M, A *is a direct answer* to $(P \mid I)$
in M iff A is a direct answer to I in M.

Example: (85) would be formalized by $(G \mid ?^1 (U, \sim U))$,
which is seen from its form to put a "conditional yes-no

question." It calls for an answer just in case the respondent is
going, and provided the respondent is going, it answers are
"*Umbrella*" and "*No umbrella.*" But if the respondent is not
going, and the concept of direct answer is therefore undefined,
then all we can say is that no answer is called for. Similarly,
(87) calls for an answer just in case the respondent has a
million dollars, and provided it calls for an answer, it answers are those to "*On what are you spending your million
dollars?*"

An important reason for putting conditions on questions is
to guard them (Åqvist 1965, p. 71): not knowing whether *I*
has a true direct answer, we may ask "If it does, please supply
one" by putting the claim that *I* has a true direct answer as a
condition on itself. For example, we may guard (57) by asking, "*If it was suicide or murder, which one was it?*":

(91) $((S\&\overline{M} \vee \overline{S}\&M) \: / \: ?^1 \forall (S, M))$.

Suppose that in fact it was neither suicide nor murder but an
accident, Then to ask (57) would be to do something "bad,"
to call for a true answer when there is none to be had. But to
ask its conditionalization (91) would be acceptable, since in
that circumstance (91) would simply be inoperative, not
calling for an answer at all.

A particularly entertaining form of this maneuver occurs
when the guarded interrogative is a *Hobson's Choice,* that is,
an interrogative with but one direct answer, as $?^1 (A)$: "Tell
me that *A.*" Let us grant that this interrogative form is of no
utility. But consider its conditionally guarded cousin, $(A \: /$
$?^1 (A))$, which calls for an answer if and only if *A* is true, and
then asks for *A.* In short, it answers to the form, "If it is true
that *A,* tell me so," the nicety of which can be seen from

examples like *"If you can't hear me clearly in the back row, tell me so."*

Conditions which arise from guarding an interrogative may be put in the general class of those conditions that are presupposed by the ingredient conditioned interrogative. Most of the concrete examples we think of in which the condition has to do generally with "the world" or "the topics of discussion" are of this sort, though of course someone could, if so minded, ask *"If snow is puce, where are the joys of yesteryear?"*, and we do in fact ask *"If there is a fire, where is the nearest exit?"* But there is an important third type of conditional interrogative which uses conditions not pertinent to the topics of discusson at all, but rather to the status of the questioner, respondent, or the information-processing situation generally: *If you have the time, tell me whether . . . . If you think I ought to know, . . . If you receive this letter before the 19th, . . .* Many of these, as well as some of the second type, make sense best when time is introduced as an explicit parameter governing when the answer is to be given: *"If there is a fire, then (i.e., literally at that time) tell me the location of the nearest exit."* But the level of abstraction at which we are currently moving does not permit us to do justice to these.

Various operations are available with which to construct new relativized interrogatives out of old ones. As illustrations we define one logical operation and one Boolean operation. In each case our task is to define the two metalinguistic locutions required for every relativized interrogative.

Suppose, first, that I has the form $I_1 \& \ldots \& I_n$, where each I_i is a relativized interrogative. Then I is a *conjunction of* these interrogatives, and (1) *I calls for an answer in M* just in case at least one of the I_i calls for an answer in M, and (2), provided I calls for an answer in M, A *is a direct answer to I in M* if and only if, where $I_{i_1}, \ldots, I_{i_r}$ is a complete list of all the interrogatives among the conjuncts of I which call for an answer in M, then A has the form $A_{i_1} \& \ldots \& A_{i_r}$, where each A_{i_k} is a direct answer in M to the matching I_{i_k}.

Suppose, second, that I has the form $I_1 \cup \ldots \cup I_n$. Then I is a *union of* these interrogatives, and A. *I calls for an answer in M* just in case at least one of the I_i calls for answer in M and B. provided I calls for an answer in M, A *is a direct answer to I in M* if and only if A is a direct answer in M to some I_i.

Consider just two examples.

(92) $(A \, /?^1(A)) \cup (B \, /?^1(B))$

is very like the single-example example question

(93) $?^1(A, B)$,

since for arbitrary C and M, C is a true direct answer in M to (92) if and only if it is so to (93). But if both A and B are false, (93) is "false" (calling for an answer, but without true answers), while (92) does not call for an answer. So (93) is a properly stronger interrogative than (92).

Second, it turns out lthat

(94) $(A \, /?^1(A)) \& (B \, /?^1(B))$

is very like the complete-list question

(95) $?\forall(A, B)$,

since, where σ is the subject of (95), a formula C is, in a given M, a true direct answer to (94) just in case $(C \, \& \, Max(C, \sigma))$ is a true direct answer to (95). But (95) has false answers, whereas (94) does not.

   Our definitions of conjunction and union of relativized interrogatives, as well as some of their definitional cousins, allow natural extension to "infinite conjunctions" and "infinite unions" via quantification into interrogatives. We leave for another occasion this as well as many other matters pertaining to questions of the new breed. (For a partial development, see Belnap 1972.)

3 Erotetic Semantics

In analogy with M. Jourdain, we have of course been talking semantics off and on from the beginning: the interrogative-question relationship is itself plainly semantical in nature, to say nothing of the truth-based concept of real alternative, etc. What makes our treatment of erotetic semantics in this section distinctive is that with a few exceptions it does not rely on the details of the erotetic grammar developed in sections one and two. Most of it is therefore applicable to a wide range of—or even all—erotetic logics.

The first business of erotetic semantics is to define rigorous analogues of some of the things we say or would like to say in informal languages about questions and answers. Indeed, we shall not in this section get much beyond this first order of business. After eliciting the foundational concepts of erotetic semantics (3.1), we provide a set of semantic concepts for cataloguing answers (3.2), a set for cataloguing interrogatives (3.3), and a set for representing relations between interrogatives (3.4). In each case, our aim has been to provide a sample rather than a survey.

We must reluctantly omit nearly all mention of the "relativized" interrogatives of 2.4, confining ourselves to the absolute variety. Where I is any such interrogative, we intend "$d(I)$," in contexts like "some $d(I)$ . . ." and "every $d(I)$ . . . ," to be understood as a common noun having as its extension the set of direct answers to I. We occasionally also use "$d(I)$" as a proper noun denoting the set of direct answers to I.

3.1 Fundamental Concepts The concept of direct answer is essential not only for the grammar but also for the semantics of questions, since the first and foundational concept of erotetic semantics is that of a question's being truly answerable, having, that is, some true direct answer. For instance, everyone knows that the wife-beating question (8) "presupposes" that John used to beat his wife, but without the concept of direct answer and of a question's being truly answerable, it is not easy to go beyond examples. Once we have the notion of direct answer isolated, however, and with the notion of true answerability, it is almost trivial that "the presupposition" of the wife-beating question can be conceptualized along with all erotetic presuppositions in an absolutely uniform way: every question presupposes precisely that at least one of its direct answers is true. (For the relativized questions of sect. 2.4, one must prefix "if it is operative, then," so as to avoid making a relativized question presuppose its own operativity.)

Let us see how this works in detail. Presupposition has had more than a run for its money in nonerotetic logic, particularly in connection with theories due to Strawson (1954). According to the technical Strawsonian use of the word "presupposition," the use of a sentence A presupposes B if the truth of B is a necessary condition for A's being successfully used to make a statement capable of being either true or false. Since we are interested only in standard uses of sentences, it is simpler to say that the sentence A itself has the presupposition B, and is itself, derivatively, if you like, either true or false when its presupposition is true. Then presupposition is to be contrasted with Tarskian logical implication: *A logically implies B* if B is a necessary condition of A's being true, while *A presupposes B* if B is a necessary condition of A's having a truth value. It is obvious that the Strawsonian notion of presupposition is only useful for a codification of language quite unlike our own in that not all sentences have truth values, in which, as Quine somewhere says, there are "truth gaps." A standard example used to illustrate the contrast is "*The present king of France is bald*," which Strawson parses in a gappy way as having a truth value only if its presupposition, that there is now a unique French king, is satisfied, and which Russell parses in a gapless way as invariably having a truth value, but as logically implying the existence of a unique French king.

This background is given in order to make the point that there is an extremely important root notion of question-presupposition which is wanted even on the present gapless view and which is more analogous to logical implication than to Strawsonian presupposition. We will use "presupposition" for sentences in the modified Strawsonian sense explained above, but for questions we reserve this word for what we take to be the more important notion. The reader imbued with Strawsonian doctrines will have to keep in mind that we are being gapless and that, therefore, the concept of question-presupposition developed below contains crucial disanalogies to the usual concepts of sentence- (or use-of-sentence-) presupposition.

Let us begin with some examples. The question (8) presupposes that John used to beat his wife. The question

(96)   *Is the present king of France bald?*

presupposes that there is now a king of France; the question

(97)   *What is the width of the desk?*

presupposes that a width is the sort of thing a desk has, and

(98)   *How fast did Jones drive down Main Street last night?*

presupposes that Jones drove down Main Street last night. Also, asking the question

(99)   *How many bones in a lion?*

ordinarily implies that the questioner doesn't know the (true) answer and thinks it likely that the respondent either knows or can find out the number of bones in a lion.

The last-mentioned relation is radically different from the others, since it describes the questioner, the respondent, and the empirical context in which the question is asked rather than the topic of the question. We may call such implications "pragmatic," since they are so closely related to the speaker involved in erotetic situations. Pragmatic implications attach not to questions bare, but to asking-questions-in-circumstances, so that it is illuminating (but only approximately true) to say that the asking of a question q in circumstance C has A as a pragmatic implicate if A is ordinarily true when q is asked in circumstance C. Since when one asks (99) in the usual information-seeking circumstances it is ordinarily true that one doesn't know the answer, we may say that the questioner's not knowing how many bones there are in a lion is in standard circumstances a pragmatic implicate of the asking of that question.

Other sorts of pragmatic implications attach more properly to a use-of-an-interrogative-in-a-circumstance than to a question, since they depend on linguistic details of the interrogative used in putting the question. We should think that the interrogative (2) puts the same question as either the interrogative *"Isn't glass a liquid at 70° F.?"* or the interrogative *"Glass is a liquid at 70°F, isn't it?"*, namely, the question as to whether or not glass is a liquid at 70°F. But in usual circumstances, the use of one of the latter interrogatives seems to imply that the questioner tends to believe, but isn't sure, that the answer should be "yes."

We are not in the sequel going to concern ourselves further with pragmatic implications of either asking a question or using an interrogative, but only with presuppositions, such as those resident in the other examples, which attach indifferently to question or interrogative and which are not descriptive of the context of interrogation.

Consider the examples again: (8) presupposes, we say, that John used to beat his wife; (96) presupposes that there is now a king of France; (97) presupposes that a width is the sort of thing a desk can have; and (98) presupposes that Jones drove down Main Street last night. Note that these presuppositions, unlike those in the "lion" example, do not describe in any specific way, the questioner, respondent, or circumstances of interrogation. That this is so can be seen by noticing that each of these questions has exactly the same presuppositions even when asked for nonstandard purposes, for example, as a test question to see if the respondent is on his toes, or as a rhetorical device when both questioner and respondent know the true answer, as often happens in the courtroom. Unlike pragmatic implications, presuppositions do not need to be relativized to circumstances.

Leonard (1957) suggests that presuppositions can be classified as either primary or secondary, so that (98) has as a primary presupposition that Jones was driving down Main Street last night, and as a secondary presupposition that there is such a place as Main Street. The idea is that the secondary presuppositions are implied by the primary, while "any presupposition which is not a secondary presupposition is called a **primary** presupposition." Sometimes, or even often, it may be useful to look at the matter in this way in attempting to assay the worth of asking or trying to answer a particular question, but still it would be nice to have a unified theory of presuppositions.

It is not only possible, but easy to formulate such a theory, given the notion of a *direct answer* to a question. Beginning with Leonard (1957), we note that he defines a presupposition of a question as "any proposition whose truth is necessary to the validity of the question." But what does it mean to say that a question is "valid"? Once we begin to think that a fruitful way of ascribing properties to questions is via the answers thereto, we are almost driven to Leonard's own account of "validity": a valid question is one "that has a correct answer." When we put these two together there emerges what seems to be the most useful concept of presupposition: A question, *q, presupposes* a statement, *A,* if and only if the truth of *A* is a logically necessary condition for there being some true answer to *q.* Evidently it is a consequence of this definition that *A* is a presupposition of *q,* if and only if every direct answer to *q* logically implies *A.* Questions have in general many presuppositions, but in spite of this we sometimes speak of "the" (unique) presupposition of a question. What we ought to have in mind in these cases is a condition which is not only necessary but also sufficient for there being some true answer, so that "the" presupposition of a question should always be that at least one of its answers is true. Less exactly, though more pointedly, a question presupposes that it can be answered truly. Usually, however, we do not pick out the metalinguistic sentence "At least one of *q*'s answers is true" in this connection, but use instead some topical sentence in the same vocabulary as *q* which is true just exactly when *q* has a true answer. The choice of the sentence we call "the presupposition" of *q* is then a mixture of semantics and grammatical convention. In order to isolate the semantical part, we may define "*A expresses-the-presupposition-of q*" by "*A* is true exactly when *q* has at least one true answer," which is to say, the truth of *A* is both sufficient and necessary for the true answerability of *q*. And we can go on to observe that in most languages one among the many *A*'s which express-the-presupposition-of *q* is (more or less) uniquely picked out by grammar as deserving of the title, "'the' (unique) presupposition of *q*."

Consider (8) with direct answers "*John has stopped beating his wife*" and "*John has not stopped beating his wife*," which we wish to interpret in a non-truth-gappy way as equivalent respectively to "*John used to beat his wife and has now stopped*" and "*John used to beat his wife and hasn't stopped*." Clearly, at least one of these sentences is true just in case "*John used to beat his wife*" is true, which is exactly why that sentence expresses-the-presupposition-of this question and is legitimately chosen by grammar as the unique presupposition of (8). Among sentences which are presupposed by this question without expressing-the-presupposition-of it are "*John is married*" and "*John used to beat someone,*" for these are necessary without being sufficient for true answerability. Similarly, (27) truly presupposes that there is at least one prime between 10 and 20, while (26) falsely presupposes that there is a unique such, and this is but to say that (27) does and (26) does not have a true answer. Further examples will spring to mind, including cases of questions, such as proper yes-no questions like (2), which are presupposition-free in the sense that it is a logical truth that at least one of their answers is true.

From the logical point of view, the wife-beating interrogative (8) is on a par with (98), which requires for there to be a true answer that for some number *n*, Jones was driving down Main Street last night at *n* miles per hour. The difference is that the style of the wife-beating interrogative wrongly suggests that it is used to put a proper yes-no question which is free of substantive presuppositions, while there is nothing

similarly misleading about the "how fast" interrogative,
which wears its presuppositions on its sleeve. So much for the
badly named "Fallacy of Many Questions."

Some writers on questions—Cohen (1929) is an example, as
is Harrah (1961), though not Harrah (1963)—speak as if they
hold that a question with a false presupposition is not a question, or that an interrogative with a false presupposition does
not succeed in putting a question. But it seems more useful
to have questions both with and without false presuppositions, just as we have statements both true and false. And
certainly we do not want to banish questions with substantive
presuppositions. We must get it out of our heads (if it was
ever there) that there is something "logically improper" in
asking *"Did you say valor or value?"* just because it is a matter of fact whether or not at least one answer is true, anymore
than there is something "logically improper" about asserting
"I said valor, not value," just because its truth or falsity is a
matter of fact. (Hiż 1962 makes a similar point.)

To ask a question with a substantive presupposition is, in
ordinary circumstances, to hold oneself responsible for the
truth of the question's presupposition and, thus, implicitly
to make a statement. Putting a question conveys information,
and we do not mean "meta-information." One can learn something "about the world" by being asked for the proportions
of sodium to chlorine in common table salt, or for the name
of the man who was seen with one's wife. Lawyers are for
this reason not supposed to ask questions which presuppose
debatable claims not yet established, for in this way they
could communicate information to the jury in illegitimate
ways.

To ask a question with a false presupposition is not like
saying something "meaningless." Rather it is very much like

making a false statement. One can do it knowingly and
maliciously, and be exactly on a par with a liar, or one can do
it innocently and be subject to exactly the same kind of
benevolent correction as a maker of false statements. For this
reason we hereby make a proposal to call a question "true" or
"false" according as its presupposition is true or false, i.e.,
according as it does or does not have some true answer.

Even though we label this a proposal and not a report of
current usage, one should not be misled by the queer sound
of "*It is true whether Freeman is Governor of Minnesota*"
(Hamblin 1963) into thinking it an excessively peculiar proposal. For surely we do call questions "sensible," "intelligent,"
"foolish," etc., in spite of never saying things like "*It is foolish whether Freeman is Governor of Minnesota.*" Still, we do
not mean to be saying that "That's a true (false) question"
has a use, but rather to be giving it a use. If this somehow
seems upsetting, pairs of locutions alternative to "true-false"
would be "valid-invalid," "answerable-unanswerable," "ad-
missible-inadmissible," and "proper-improper." (Note that in
this sense of "answerable," a question is answerable if and
only if it is truly answerable. And let the reader be warned
that further on we introduce "answerable" with quite a different sense.) Or one can avoid predicating anything directly of
the question by referring always to its presupposition.

In order to avoid confusion, let us mention that Åqvist
(1965) also predicates truth and falsehood of questions, but
with a radically different meaning. As we interpret him, to
say of a question that it is true in his sense means not just
that the question is truly answerable but that it ought to be
answered. Since presumably one need not answer a question
which is false in our sense, truth in his sense implies truth in
ours, but not conversely. Among the reasons recommending

our usage over his is that it lines up "truth" with the factual matter of true answerability instead of with the normative matter of whether or not the question ought to be answered.

The above account of presuppositions of questions has nothing to do with Strawsonian presuppositions, since it makes sense for the gapless codification of language, while the latter has to do with truth gaps. Erotetic presupposition as described above is instead an analogue to standard logical implication. Suppose, however, we consider a truth-gappy codification of language, with A being a Strawsonian presupposition of B if the truth of A is required for B's having a truth value. Then we could define Strawsonian presupposition for questions by the formula, *q S-presupposes A* if and only if the truth of A is required for at least one direct answer to q to have a truth value. That is, A is an S-presupposition of q if and only if A is a Strawsonian presupposition of each answer to q, just as A is a presupposition of q just in case A is a logical consequence of each answer to q. It will turn out that questions like "*Is the present king of France bald?*" have exactly the same *S-presuppositions* when giving their answers a truth-gappy reading as they have *presuppositions* on the gapless interpretation, which is probably a good thing.

But it can also be misleading, for, if one pays attention only to these special cases, one will overlook some fundamental disanalogies. To bring these out we need a clear-cut example of a question whose answers are free of Strawsonian presuppositions. This is not so easy, since so many English sentences have Strawsonian presuppositions. Simple existential sentences, however, are in their standard uses said to be presupposition free, so we can take as our example something like "*Which of the following exist: unicorns or chimeras?*", with answers "*Unicorns exist*" and "*Chimeras exist.*" Here there are no Strawsonian presuppositions, but still the question quite obviously presupposes "*Either unicorns or chimeras exist*," that is, that at least one of the answers is true. This example shows that it would be wrong to take over too directly into erotetic logic the Strawsonian notion of presupposition for assertoric logic, saying something like "the use of an interrogative presupposes *A* if the truth of *A* is required for the interrogative to be used to ask a question." Clearly, the unicorn-chimera interrogative can be used to put an answerable question—even if answers are taken to be statements and not sentences—regardless of whether or not its presupposition is true. Of course, the question put cannot be answered truly, but in spite of having a false presupposition, it can certainly be answered truly-or-falsely.

There is a variation of *S*-presupposition which some might prefer: let us say that a question, *q*, *S*-presupposes A* just in case the truth of *A* is required for it to be the case that all of *q*'s direct answers have a truth value. Then "*Of the present king of France and the present king of England, which one is bald?*" would *S**-presuppose the existence of a French king, but it would *S*-presuppose only the existence of at least one of a French or an English king.

Our discussion has been framed so as to have relevance to natural languages as well as to our formal erotetic logic. We now turn to putting the matter formally. In what ensues we shall in the formal definitions uniformly attach presuppositions and other concepts to interrogatives instead of to questions, leaving it to the reader to see that producing the parallel definitions for questions would be straightforward. But we shall continue to talk about questions in some of the descriptive passages.

As one might expect, the story has to be complicated somewhat for which-interrogatives in order to take into account the way such an interrogative can have "real answers" (in the sense of sect. 1.34) which are not signified by any direct answer. Because of this, it is possible for an interrogative such as (76) to have a true real answer but no true direct answer, hence to puzzle us as to whether we should call its presupposition true or false, and, accordingly, as to whether we should pay attention to real or direct answers in articulating the concept of presupposition through true answerability.

The puzzle is to a certain extent resolved by defining two notions of truth (i.e., true answerability) and two notions of presupposition for which-interrogatives, one of the "real" and one of the "nominal" variety. For A a formula, I a which-interrogative, and M an interpretation, I is *really true* [*really false*] in M iff some real answer to I is true in M [every real answer to I is false in M]; I is *nominally true* [*nominally false*] in M iff some (nominal) $d(I)$ is true in M [every $d(I)$ is false in M]; I *really* [*nominally*] *presupposes A* iff A is true in every M in which I is really [nominally] true; and A *expresses-the-real-* [*nominal-*] *presupposition* of I iff A is true in exactly those interpretations in which I is really [nominally] true. (Recall that $d(I)$" is short for "direct answer to I.")

For whether-interrogatives we need only, of course, say that I is *true in M* iff some $d(I)$ is true in M, and is otherwise *false* in M; that I *presupposes A* if A is true in every M in which I is true; and that A *expresses-the-presupposition-of I* if true in exactly those M in which I is true.

In Belnap (1963), truth (without qualification) for which-interrogatives was identified with nominal truth, and similarly for presupposition. But in harmony with our discussion of (76) in section 1.34 and with our treatment of completeness-claims in section 1.32, it now seems to us best to go the other way, choosing real truth and real presupposition as "real" truth and presupposition. We shall, therefore, use the unqualified "*I is true in M*," "*I presupposes A*," and "*A expresses-the-presupposition-of I*" for which- as well as for whether-interrogatives, meaning for which-interrogatives always the "real" variety.

There is in general no guarantee that there will exist any formulas which express-the-presupposition-of a given interrogative *I*, but in fact for each elementary interrogative there is such a formula. And since there is one, it follows by the usual logical equivalences that there are many, which is why we do not say in the definitions above that *A* is *the* presupposition of *I*. For some purposes, however, it is useful to follow the lead of natural language and choose by grammatical convention a particular formula, *Pres(I)*, as in a privileged way being (and not just expressing) the presupposition of *I*. The method of choice is obvious for *I* a whether-interrogative. One simply selects some convenient disjunction of the direct answers to *I*, which must perforce be true if and only if *I* has some true direct answer. The task for which-questions is not quite as easy, but rather than carry it out, we allow an informally worked out example to suffice. Let *I* be the which-interrogative $?\rho(Cx \mathbin{/\!/} Fx)$. Then the presupposition of *I* will contain from one to three conjuncts, $P_1 \& P_2 \& P_3$, as follows. P_1 is always present, and says that at least one *C* is an *F*. P_2 is present just in case (i) ρ has the form $\binom{v}{u} \forall \mathbf{d}$) instead of $\binom{v}{u} - \mathbf{d}$), and (ii) v is an integer instead of "–". And when present, P_2 says that at most v *C*'s are *F*'s. P_3 is present just in case ρ has the form $\binom{v}{u} \mathbf{c} \neq$) instead of $\binom{v}{u} \mathbf{c} -$), and, when present, P_3 says that at least u *C*'s are *F*'s. (Of course the presence of P_3 makes P_1 redundant.)

Since the formal details are not illuminating, we omit them altogether, supposing that the formal job is done and that for each elementary interrogative, *I*, *Pres(I)*—*the presupposition of I*—is an effectively specified formula which expresses-the-presupposition-of *I*.

We note in passing that it is not in general possible to find for each which-interrogative *I* a formula which expresses-the-*nominal*-presupposition-of *I*. Belnap (1963), section 7.5, contains a detailed discussion of this failure, a failure which supplies us with one reason for identifying "presupposition" with "real presupposition" instead of "nominal presupposition".

In section 1.0 we mentioned the various standard semantic concepts amenable to definition in terms of truth. We will rehearse the definitions here since they are to play an important role in what follows. It is to be noted that since we have given a meaning, and a good one, to the application of "true" and "false" to interrogatives, it makes sense to extend the other semantic concepts to cover interrogatives as well as formulas. It was in fact partly to make this extension easy that we opted for the pair "true-false" as among such other candidates as "answerable-unanswerable," and in exactly the same spirit we now baptize interrogatives and formulas alike as *quasi formulas,* and use *X* and *H* as ranging respectively over quasi formulas and sets of quasi formulas. By this much it would seem that we are favoring the poet over the philosopher in the titular dispute raised by juxtaposing the title "Questions aren't statements" of Hamblin 1963 with the title "A question is a statement" of a Wallace Stevens poem, but of course our true view is somewhere in between. A question is in part a statement, or as we shall say, an interrogative has "propositional content." It is exactly in virtue of this propositional content that an interrogative can enter into semantic relationships ordinarily thought of as reserved for statements alone.

The definitions which follow are thoroughly orthodox, except for the extension to all quasi formulas, including interrogatives, and except for occasional use of "propositional" as a prefix in order to remind us that it is only the propositional content of an interrogative which counts in determining whether or not it enters into the defined relationship. M, as usual, ranges over interpretations.

M *is an H-interpretation* iff every quasi formula in H is true in M.

X is *logically H-true, H-consistent,* or *H-inconsistent,* according as X is true in all, some, or no H-interpretations. Also, X is *H-inconsistent* with X' if both are never simultaneously true in the same H-interpretation, and X is *H-consistent with X'* if both are simultaneously true in some H-interpretation.

Above and below the same definitions hold with "H-" systematically dropped throughout.

A quasi formlula X' [or a set of quasi formulas H'] *propositionally H-implies* a quasi formula X iff X is true in every H-interpretation in which X' [or every member of H'] is true. If X and X' propositionally H-imply each other and are hence true in exactly the same H-interpretations, they are said to be *propositionally H-equivalent.*

In former publications, for instance, Belnap (1963), we used "logically equivalent" for "propositionally equivalent," and similarly for "implies," since these phrases with "logical" are in almost universal use among nonerotetic ("assertoric") logicians. But that usage led us to say apparently peculiar things like "every interrogative is logically equivalent to its own presupposition"—obviously I and *Pres(I)* are true in exactly the same interpretations—which misleadingly suggested that an interrogative and its presupposition should be interchangeable from every logical point of view, including that of erotetic logic. Regardless of the phrases used, no misunderstanding can ensue if one remembers the definitions. But it is obviously best to use when possible the least misleading terminology available. Thus our decision to save "logically equivalent" for some notion of equivalence-with-no-holds-barred, using "propositional equivalence" for equivalence-of-propositional-content. And it does not sound terribly odd to say that *Pres(I)* propositionally implies and indeed is propositionally equivalent to *I*.

Since the modifier "propositionally" is helpful only when one of the terms of the relation is an interrogative, we shall sometimes omit it in application to formulas, saying "*A* implies *B*" or "*A* is equivalent to *B*."

In spite of everything, some may remain nervous about the very idea of a quasi formula. Any such person can in all of the above definitions substitute *Pres(I)*—the grammatically defined presupposition of *I*—for *I* itself, since of course these two have always exactly the same truth value, so that *Pres(I)* expresses exactly the propositional content of *I*. But such a person should be aware (i) that this substitution is only possible when *Pres(I)* is defined, as it is for elementary interrogatives, (ii) that such a substitution would tend to obscure the fact that the considerations and concepts articulated below are quite independent of whether or not grammatical chance, or design, has found a *Pres(I)* for every *I,* and (iii) that in any event something like the concept of the "propositional content" of an interrogative is required in order to justify semantically any choice of *Pres(I)*.

The set of quasi formulas *H* to which we relativize various concepts can often usefully be thought of as the set of axioms of some formal theory. In the definitions given below, however, it is sometimes convenient to think of H as representing the set of statements and interrogatives which the questioner, or respondent, knows or believes to be true. Of course, the definitions themselves are perfectly meaningful independently of any of these heuristic devices. It is, rather, their point which depends on how H is construed.

It is to be noted that, given the above definitions, presupposition is not only analogous to but identical with propositional implication: I presupposes A if and only if I propositionally implies A. And, of course, A expresses-the-presupposition-of I if and only if A is propositionally equivalent to I. We shall feel free to express these relationships in whichever words seem appropriate.

The first and most fundamental consequence of the definitions given so far is this: each interrogative I is, insofar as it has propositional content, propositionally implied by each of its direct answers. For if such an answer is true in M, then a fortiori some $d(I)$ is true in M, hence some real answer is true in M, so that I is true in M. Equivalently, when $Pres(I)$ is defined), every $d(I)$ implies $Pres(I)$.

We now turn to the task of applying these definitions in an analysis of concepts useful in appraising or categorizing questions and answers. The phrases we shall be defining will be of use to anyone who wishes to go beyond firsthand participation in question-answer situations in order to make metalinguistic comments about the proceedings in which they or others may be involved. Indeed, it seems to us plain that any sufficiently well developed question-answering or question-asking capability—whether artificial or not—should most certainly have at its disposal at least the following concepts for use in making and receiving remarks about its own performance. We shall first develop some concepts applicable to answers, then a few applicable to questions, and, finally, we shall define a sample of question-question relationships.

3.2 Cataloguing Answers   Responses to an interrogative can, in the first place, be categorized according to their gross semantic relations to (the propositional content of) the interrogative. We shall say that a formula, considered as a response to *I*, is *H-uninformative* if it is propositionally *H*-implied by *I* (or, if you prefer, by *Pres(I)*), and otherwise that it is *H-informative*. And we shall say that a formula so taken is *H-foolish* if it is *H*-inconsistent, and otherwise that it is *H-possible*. Also, we call a formula *relatively H-foolish* if it is *H*-inconsistent with *I*, and otherwise *relatively H-possible*. (This is a distinction without a difference for direct answers.)

Example: Let *I* be

(100) $?^1(A \lor B, C\&D)$,

where *A, B, C,* and *D* have no special properties or relations, and let *F* be a similarly commonplace but otherwise arbitrary formula. Then $(A \lor B) \lor (C\&D) \lor F$ is uninformative and both possible and relatively possible, while its denial is informative and relatively foolish, but not foolish. The formula *A* by itself is both possible and informative, as is *F*. If *I* is consistent, then "uninformative" implies both "possible" and "relatively possible," and both "foolish" and "relatively foolish" imply "informative," but these implications fail for inconsistent interrogatives.

   In order to obtain a less crude and more distinctively erotetic categorization, we must have recourse to the notion of direct answer. The guiding idea is that there are many statements which, though not direct answers, nevertheless stand in

sufficiently interesting semantic relations to direct answers
that these statements themselves by this indirect route come
to deserve the rubric "answer." Although a number of useful
and illuminating distinctions are available with respect to the
various sorts of answers, we here confine ourselves to a small
selection.

Given an interrogative I, a formula A, and a set of quasi
formulas H, we will say that A is an *H-complete answer* to I
iff A H-implies some $d(I)$; an *H-just-complete answer* iff A is
H-equivalent to some $d(I)$; an *H-partial answer* iff A is H-
implied by some $d(I)$; an *H-eliminative answer* iff A H-implies
the denial of some $d(I)$; and an *H-quasi-eliminative answer* iff
A is H-implied by the denial of some $d(I)$.

Examples: Let I again be (100). Then A and B are complete answers, since they imply the direct answer $A \lor B$; $B \lor A$
is a just-complete answer since equivalent to $A \lor B$, C and D
are partial answers since implied by the direct answer $C \& D$,
$\bar{C}$ and $\bar{D}$ are eliminative answers since implying the denial of
$C \& D$, $\bar{A}$ and $\bar{B}$ are quasi-eliminative answers since implied by
the denial of $A \lor B$. Receiving a complete answer is sufficient
for the perfect logician, though of course such an answer can
contain irrelevant information: *"Glass is a liquid at 70° F.,
and China is populous"* is a complete answer to (2). Just-
complete answers are interchangeable with direct answers for
the perfect logician, but not for the rest of us. We remind the
reader that he must resist the temptation to define "direct
answer" in such a way that *every* just-complete answer is a
direct answer, since propositional equivalence is not an effectively decidable relation, just-complete answerhood is not
effectively decidable either, while direct answerhood must be
effective. (See 1.34.) Relative to the usual arithmetical

assumptions, "*Glass is a liquid at $(2^6 + 6)° F.$*" is a just-complete answer to (2). Partial answers tend in the usual cases to give inductive evidence for the direct answer or answers by which they are implied. Their semantic information content is "part" of that of some direct answer. "*Her ladyship was wearing emeralds*" is a partial answer to (56). The negation of a partial answer is invariably an eliminative answer. Such an answer eliminates as a live option the direct answer (or answers) the negation of which it implies. "*Her ladyship wasn't wearing any emeralds*" is an eliminative answer to (56). The negation of a complete answer is a quasi-eliminative answer. Just as a partial answer tends to give inductive evidence for the truth of a direct answer by which it is implied, so a quasi-eliminative answer tends to give inductive evidence for the falsity of a direct answer by the negation of which it is implied. "*He wasn't murdered by the butler*" is a quasi-eliminative answer to (57).

Given (100), it is apparent that $(A \lor B)\&F$ (with F arbitrary) is a complete answer in some sense in which $T \supset (A \lor B)$ (with T some long and complicated formula involving quantifiers which happens to be logically true) is not. If the respondent gives the questioner $(A \lor B)\&F$ he can *easily* derive the direct answer $A \lor B$, but to obtain this from $T \supset (A \lor B)$ he would first have to establish that T is logically true, a task to which he may not be equal. The difference between these cases is real, but one which cannot be handled by semantics. We would have to step up to pragmatics (or across to proof theory), introducing a parameter K that referred to a set of methods of derivation. Then we would define "complete, relative to the set of methods K," and it would turn out that for an interesting K, $(A \lor B)\&F$ would be a complete answer to (100) but $T \supset (A \lor B)$ would not. This suggestion may lead to little of theoretical interest, but it would be of enormous use in applications to artificial query systems. We take this opportunity to observe that relativization to methods of derivation is applicable also to a number of the concepts defined below, especially to the concepts *answerable* and *moot.*

An important variation on one of the above definitions is due, in essence, to Harrah (1961). Let us say that A is a *Harrah-H-complete answer* to I if A is a $(H \cup \{I\})$-complete answer to I. The idea is that in the ordinary situation the questioner will believe his question to be true and will hence be willing to treat the propositional content of his question as part of the background knowledge relative to which the completeness of answers is defined. Where I is (100), $\bar{C}$ and $\bar{D}$, though not complete answers, are both Harrah-complete answers, since together with (the propositional content of) I, each implies $A \lor B$; that is, each $\{I\}$- implies $A \lor B$. (If at least one answer is true, and it is not the second, it must be the first.) Similarly, "*11 is a prime lying between 10 and 20*" is a Harrah-complete answer to (26), since, together with (the propositional content of) (26), it propositionally implies the required completeness-claim. And speaking generally, if I is a unique-alternative interrogative, then every alternative presented by the subject of I is a Harrah-complete answer to I.

Among partial answers, those which are implied by some H-consistent $d(I)$ are called *proper H-partial answers.* Suppose one wanted to ask a "test-question" (Harrah 1963, p. 37), one of the answers to which is inconsistent, for example, $?^1(A \& \bar{A}, B)$. Then, since $A \& \bar{A}$ implies every statement whatsoever, every statement counts as a partial answer to this interrogative. But only the implicates of B would be proper partial answers.

Some partial answers are of little use in that they are not H-informative. Such partial answers can give no evidence in favor of one direct answer over another, since they are implied equally by all. For instance, SVM is hardly helpful with respect to $?^1(S, M)$: "Was it suicide or murder?" "Well, it was one or the other." (Harrah has suggested calling such an answer—an uninformative partial answer—a *safe* answer.) Clearly, helpful partial answers will have to be a both proper and informative. We therefore say that A is a *highly proper H-partial answer* if A is both *H*-informative and a proper *H*-partial answer. If A is a highly proper partial answer to I, then to know both $Pres(I)$ and A is to know more than $Pres(I)$, but no more than some consistent $d(I)$: the conjunction of $Pres(I)$ with A has an information content properly containing that of I and (properly or improperly) contained by that of some consistent $d(I)$. In the scheme of Harrah (1963), it is in effect highly proper partial answers which must be paid for.

Among the eliminative answers to an interrogative I there are some which are of special interest for erotetic logic, to wit, those that eliminate every direct answer to I. Evidently if such a formula is true, the interrogative I must be nominally false, so that to respond with such a formula is to charge the questioner with harboring a false nominal presupposition. To thus respond is therefore to *correct* the questioner. We are consequently led to define a formula A as a *nominal H-corrective answer* to I iff A implies the denial of every $d(I)$. And making the now familiar move from the nominal to the real, we also define A as an *H-corrective answer* to I iff I is (really) false in every M in which A is true.

A corrective answer which corrects I but does no more than that is called a "just corrective answer": A is a *just H-corrective answer* to I iff A is true in exactly those M in which I is false. Sometimes grammar chooses one among the just-corrective answers, which we may think of as *the standard correction to I*. The standard correction to (8) is doubtless something like "*John has never beaten his wife.*" For our formal language, we follow Åqvist in using "*Corr(I)*" for the standard correction to *I*, which we define for elementary interrogatives as $\overline{Pres(I)}$. *Corr(I)* is a just-corrective answer to *I,* so that our definition is semantically justified.

Formulas (not interrogatives) which stand in any one of the above defined relations to an interrogative *I* relative to a set of quasi formulas *H* will be said to be *erotetically H-relevant* to *I.* The reader will be able to think of formulas which with respect to a given interrogative are erotetically relevant without being informative and of other formulas which are informative without being erotetically relevant. We remark in passing that on these definitions both inconsistencies and logical truths turn out to be erotetically relevant to every interrogative, an anomaly which is to be debited to the account of the orthodox concept of propositional implication and which could be avoided by using in its place the notion of "entailment" of Anderson and Belnap (1975). In any case, the feeling of oddity is perhaps lessened by observing that, though inconsistencies and logical truths are erotetically relevant to an arbitrary interrogative, the former are still foolish and the latter uninformative.

3.3 *Cataloguing Interrogatives* We turn now to a set of semantically defined concepts applicable to interrogatives, the first four falling naturally into a "square of opposition": an interrogative *I* is *H-safe* iff *I* (qua quasi formula, or *Pres(I)* if that is defined) is logically *H*-true, that is, propositionally implied by *H.* Otherwise, *I* is *H-risky.* And *I* is *H-foolish* iff *H*-inconsistent, and otherwise it is *H-possible.*

The notion of safety is due to Harrah. The importance of a safe interrogative is that it can be answered truly no matter what the state of the universe. An interrogative like (2) having the proper yes-no form $?^1(A, \bar{A})$ is invariably safe, since in every M one of the answers must be true. And an improper yes-no interrogative (8) having the form $?^1$ ($B\&S, B\&\bar{S}$), though risky, will be H-safe if H contains B. The unique-alternative interrogative $?^1 \forall(Nx \; // \; 7+5 = x)$ is H-safe for H the ordinary assumptions of arithmetic, which guarantee a uniquely true answer to this interrogative. But it is not safe to ask $?^1 \forall(Nx \; // \; (y) (x > y))$, that is, *"What is the largest number?"* Indeed, though the question is possible in the absolute sense, it is H-foolish where H codifies arithmetic. (8) is both risky and possible, but it would be H-safe if H contained *"John has beaten his wife,"* and H-foolish if H contained *"John has never beaten his wife."* More generally, I is H-safe if H contains or propositionally implies $Pres(I)$, and I is H-foolish if H contains or propositionally implies the standard correction to I, $Corr(I)$.

Note that a risky interrogative can turn out to be true (in the principal interpretation), and a possible interrogative can turn out to be false.

All of these interrogative-cataloguing concepts have important nominal variants, and all have variants for questions. When the latter variants are considered, one discovers that it is foolish to ask a foolish question since every direct answer is false. As a matter of fact, this observation can be strengthened inasmuch as we have the following as a consequence of our definitions:

Theorem: *Ask a foolish question and you get a foolish answer.*

Friends have urged that we take credit for this theorem— it is perhaps the *Haupstatz* of erotetic semantics— on the grounds that we are the first to publish its proof. But although we are sensitive to the compliment, scholarship bids us call attention to an anticipation of the result by a logician of India:

> In this voyage [Alexander the Great] took ten of the Indian philosophers prisoners . . . These men because they go stark naked, are called Gymnosophists, and are reputed to be extremely sharp and succinct in their answers to whatsoever is propounded to them, which [Alexander] made trial of, by putting difficult questions to them, withal letting them know, that those whose answers were not pertinent, should be put to death . . . Of the fifth [gymnosophist] he asked, *Which was eldest, Night or Day?* The philosopher replied, *Day was eldest, by one day at least*; but perceiving Alexander not well satisfied with that account, he added, *that he ought not to wonder, if strange questions had as odd answers made to them.* (Plutarch *Lives*.)

Standard mathematical practice christens a theorem by the name of the man who first conjectures its truth, consigning to oblivion the fellow who later manages by dint of hard work to produce a rigorous proof. So, with reluctant cheerfulness, we urge that the proposition whose proof first appears below be known as "The Theorem of the Fifth Gymnosophist."

   Proof: We give the proof for interrogatives. Suppose for *reductio* that there were a foolish I such that some direct answer to I, say A, were not foolish. Then A would not be inconsistent, so that A would be true in some interpretation M. But then I would have a true answer, namely A, in that M.

Hence I would be true in M, hence true in some interpretation, so not inconsistent, so not foolish, contrary to hypothesis. We must therefore give up the supposition of the *reductio*. *Q.E.D.*

Of course, it can even be foolish to ask a true question. The following example is due to Nicholas Rescher: although (given the temporal finitude of the English language) there *is* a true answer to *"What is an example of an integer, the name of which neither has been, is being, nor will be produced by anyone?"* still, it is not possible to give a true direct answer to this question.

One particularly foolish sort of interrogative is called "dumb": I is a *dumb interrogative* iff I has no direct answers whatsoever. If one traces through our definitions one will find that an interrogative like $?(^-_3 - -)(A, B)$ is dumb in this sense: *"What are at least three truths from among the following: A and B?"* has no answers. That our erotetic logic allows such interrogatives may be construed by some as perhaps a defect, but, as in the case of such formal oddities as vacuous quantification, it is easier to admit them than it is to go to the trouble of explicitly ruling them out.

Still further useful semantic characterizations of interrogatives are possible, among which is the idea of an interrogative's being "exclusive" in the sense that the truth of any one of its answers excludes the truth of all the others. Let us say that I is *H-exclusive* if in each H-interpretation there is at most one true real answer (for which-interrogatives) or abstract answer (for whether-interrogatives). Then unique-alternative whether- and which-interrogatives turn out to be exclusive as expected, as do complete-list whether-interrogatives. No other interrogative of these specially named in 1.34 is guaranteed exclusive by its erotetic form alone. However, let us say that two real answers are *permutation-equivalent* if the sequenced selection of one is a permutation of that of the other, and that a which-interrogative I is *H-permutation-exclusive* if in no H-interpretation are there as many as two non-permutation-equivalent real answers. Then complete-and-distinct-list which-interrogatives are permutation-exclusive, but complete-list which-interrogatives need not be. However, let us say that two real answers are *set-equivalent* if they are alike in the set of alternatives appearing in their sequenced selections, and that a which-interrogative I is *H-set-exclusive* if in no H-interpretation are there as many as two non-set-equivalent real answers. Then complete-list which-questions are set-exclusive. Further, let us say that I is *nominally H-exclusive* if in each H-interpretation at most one $d(I)$ is true. Then of the six named forms, only the unique-alternative whether-interrogative is nominally exclusive. However, if we say that I is *weakly nominally H-exclusive* if distinct $d(I)$ are either H-logically equivalent or H-inconsistent (so that if several $d(I)$ to a weakly nominally H-exclusive interrogative are true then they are all H-logically equivalent), then complete-list whether-questions turn out to be weakly nominally exclusive. Theorem 7.16 of Harrah (1963) gives a result related to weak exclusivity.

We shall further say that an interrogative I *is answerable by* a set of quasi formulas H if H propositionally implies some $d(I)$, and otherwise that I is *H-unanswerable*. These concepts have Harrah versions: I *is Harrah-answerable* by H if $H \cup \{I\}$ propositionally implies some $d(I)$. But when we are thinking of H as representing the knowledge or beliefs of the questioner rather than the respondent, then instead of saying that I is Harrah-answerable by H, we can say that I *is H-rhetorical,* in that sense in which to say that I is rhetorical is to say that it is self-answering. And instead of Harrah-unanswerable by H, we can say that I is *H-moot* or *H-open.* One would expect the questioner in the typical erotetic situation to believe that his interrogative is moot relative to the information at his own disposal but answerable by the information at the disposal of the respondent. If the questioner is mistaken about this latter point, then it is open to the respondent to reply with "I don't know," which seems best construed as shorthand for the metalinguistic remark, "your interrogative is not answerable by the set of formulas representing the information at my disposal."

Although in general one cannot effectively tell whether or not a given interrogative is rhetorical, there is one sort of interrogative which is obviously rhetorical in virtue of its form alone, a *Hobson's Choice,* that is, an interrogative with but one direct answer. Examples would be $?^1(A)$, and also $?^1(Cx \mathbin{/\!/} Fx)$, provided there is only one name in the nominal category determined by the category condition Cx. We make no special plea for the usefulness of this sort of interrogative, only claiming to have given rigor to a concept dating back to 1712. (But see sect. 2.4.) Standing towards the other end of the scale from a Hobson's Choice is an interrogative I to which H provides neither a Harrah-complete answer nor an eliminative answer. In this case I might well be called *hyper-H-moot* or *H-wide-open,* since for such an interrogative, every $d(I)$ is a "live option" in the sense that neither its truth nor its falsity is a propositional consequence of $H \cup \{I\}$. When H represents the questioner's beliefs, there is something a bit odd about any interrogative he uses which is not hyper-H-moot, but of course he may well have his reasons for tolerating such oddities.

Åqvist (1965, p. 56) suggests calling an interrogative "nor-

mal" if no answer is implied by another. We do not adopt the
terminology, because it suggests that it might be "abnormal"
to ask a some-examples question like $?_1^-$ (A, B, C), the point
of which we defend on the grounds that the questioner may
place higher value on answers with more information, such as
$A \& B$ than he does on either A or B (see sect. 1.31). But the
concept is interesting. Let us say an interrogative I is *H-inde-
pendent* if no $d(I)$ *H*-implies any distinct $d(I)$. An even
stronger concept is that of *H-minimality*: I is said to be *H-
minimal* if the deletion of even one direct answer would
strengthen its presupposition. This could be stated precisely
in terms of the concept of difference of interrogatives (sect.
2.31), or equivalently as follows: I is *H*-minimal if for every
A which is a $d(I)$, there is an *H*-interpretation M in which A
is the sole true answer to I, that is, in which A is true while
every other $d(I)$ is false. Evidently, minimality implies independence, but not conversely. For example, $?^1 (A, \overline{A}, B)$ is
independent, but it is not minimal since there is no M in
which B is the sole true answer.

3.4 Relations between Interrogatives The most important semantic relation between interrogatives is perhaps "containment,"
that relation which obtains between two interrogatives when
any answer to the first provides—for a perfect logician—an
answer to the second. The simplest definition for absolute
interrogatives is to say that I_1 *H-contains* I_2 just in case every
$d(I_1)$ is an *H*-complete answer to I_2. In order that foolish interrogatives will contain dumb ones, however, we say instead
"every *H-consistent* $d(I_1)$ . . . ." Note that if the set $d(I_1)$
set-theoretically contains the set $d(I_2)$, then the erotetic relation goes the other way: I_2 contains I_1. For example, no
matter how $?^1 (A, B)$ is answered, one is bound to have an
answer to $?^1 (A, B, C)$, but not conversely. If I_2 is *H*-safe but

I_1 is not, then it might sometimes be better to ask I_2 instead of I_1 even when I_1 *H*-contains I_2. But if I is *H*-safe, then, for the perfect logician knowing H, it seems fair to say that I puts at least as good as question as does any interrogative it *H*-contains, provided one's sole motive is to obtain some-answer-or-other and one does not put different values on the answers to the contained interrogative. We return to this in a moment.

There is an important Harrah version of containment: I_1 *Harrah-H-contains* I_2 if whenever A is a $d(I_1)$, A is a Harrah-*H*-complete answer to I_2. A perfect logician who believes the presupposition of I_2 can then obtain a desired answer by asking I_1 instead, if I_1 Harrah-contains I_2. For example $?^1(A, B)$ Harrah-contains $?^1 \forall (A, B)$, so that when one believes the exactly-one-is-true presupposition of the latter, one can ask the former instead.

Mutual containment might be thought to be the best candidate for the concept of "erotetic equivalence"—equivalence no-holds-barred—but it will not do if one accepts the usefulness of nonminimal interrogatives. For $?(^1_1 - -) (A, B)$ and $?(^-_1 - -) (A, B)$ contain each other, but even the perfect logician will prefer the latter if he values the information of $A \& B$ above that of either A or B. On the other hand, if two interrogatives have exactly equivalent answers, then they would seem to be interchangeable by a perfect logician for all erotetic prupsoes. And so we define I_1 as *erotetically H-equivalent* to I_2 if for every $d(I_1)$ there is an *H*-equivalent $d(I_2)$, and for every $d(I_2)$ there is an *H*-equivalent $d(I_1)$. So if I_1 and I_2 are erotetically equivalent, the answers to each can be partitioned by propositional equivalence into exactly the same set of equivalence classes, which is all the perfect logician ever cares about.

The Harrah version takes into account the presuppositions

of both interrogatives: I_1 is *Harrah-erotetically H-equivalent*
to I_2 if and only if I_1 is erotetically ($\{I_1, I_2\} \cup H$)-equivalent
to I_2. One sees that $?^1(A, B)$ and $?^1 \forall (A, B)$ are Harrah-
erotetically equivalent in this sense.

The usefulness of the concepts of containment and equivalence is obvious for the planning of question campaigns and
the like. We add three further concepts with like employment.
First, a sequence of interrogatives $(I_1, \ldots, I_n)$ is said to be a
direct partition of an interrogative I if the conjunctive interrogative $I_1 \& \ldots \& I_n$ (see sect. 2.32) is erotetically equivalent
to I, and a *subdirect partition* if $I_1 \& \ldots \& I_n$ is erotetically
equivalent to $\overbrace{I \& \ldots \& I}^{n \text{ times}}$. Note that the sequence (I, I) is only
a subdirect partition and not in general also a partition of I.

Second, having defined in section 3.2 the locution "*A* is
erotetically relevant to I," with A a formula, we may now
define "I_1 *is erotetically relevant to* I_2," with I_2 an interrogative, by the requirement that some $d(I_1)$ be erotetically relevant to I_2. Examples of pairs like $?^1(A, \bar{A})$ and $?^1(B, \bar{B})$ show
that propositionally equivalent interrogatives can neverthe-
less lack erotetic relevance.

Lastly, we say that I_1 *H-obviates* I_2 if every $d(I_1)$ is either
an *H*-corrective answer or an *H*-complete answer to I_2. For in
that case, obtaining an answer to I_1 makes unnecessary the
asking of I_2, since each answer to the former either provides
us with an answer to I_2 or tells us that there is none to be
had.

Example: The two-answer interrogative "*Is this the end of
this essay or is there one more section to come?*" obviates,
relative to some obvious assumptions, "*How many more sections are to come?*"

4   Possible Applications

Our motivation for embarking upon an investigation of the principles of erotetic logic was sparked by three interests: one intellectual, one technological, and one social. First, as might be expected, is the intellectual interest intrinsic in developing a subject that has long been deprecated in favor of its partner in the analysis of linguistic apparatus, assertoric logic. A second, equally persuasive, aspect of our motivation is the current pressing need for an understanding of the question-answer relationship to provide a theoretical foundation for the development of new technology essential to important data processing applications. These applications, called "data base management systems," are currently generating considerable public concern over their potential for permitting inappropriate government, as well as private, surveillance and attendant invasion of personal privacy. This situation provides our third motivation for continued pursuit of the study of erotetic logic. As we will discuss below, erotetic logic may provide the only method of permitting the full, legitimate use of data-base systems in an environment that provides some guarantee of protection against illegitimate use.

The intrinsic intellectual motivation requires no elaboration to those disposed to read an account such as this. In the present instance, however, there is the additional stimulus of the prevailing view of most older logicians that erotetic logic is an essentially sterile enterprise. We are convinced that this view is erroneous. Our conviction is due in no small measure to our belief that this presumption of sterility is a consequence of a classical overemphasis on "yes-no" questions. While such questions have an obvious significance, they are, as we have shown, only a special case of a much richer repertoire of possible interrogative forms.

Beyond purely intellectual interest in erotetic logic qua logic lies an ever more compelling need for an understanding of the question-answer relationship as it is exposed in data-processing applications. The data-processing industry has undergone explosive growth in the past three decades, expanding from nothing to a $50 billion per year business. Recent studies (Dolotta et al 1976) provide persuasive evidence that this growth will continue at a comparable rate for the foreseeable future, reaching a volume of $200 billion per year by 1985. This figure is in excess of 15% of the expected gross national product of the United States at that time and makes it likely that the data-processing industry will be the largest extant business within a decade. A concomitant of this growth is the spread of data-processing applications into virtually every sphere of human activity, a process which also shows no sign of slowing. The social and economic consequences of this phenomenon are obviously considerable. It should be evident that a thorough understanding of the fundamental principles of the subject is most desirable. The fact is, however, that no such understanding exists. The entire subject of data processing is, in some sense, a castle built of sand.

Most modern technology has a firm theoretical base, even if some extreme applications are based on ill-understood phenomena. In general, the coupling between fundamental science and application is direct and soundly based, examples being physics-engineering and biochemistry-medicine. Further, the mathematics upon which these fundamental, hard sciences are based is generally well developed and widely understood. Much of the science and mathematics is more than a century old despite the rapid advances in recent years of the physical sciences. This is particularly true of the mathematics used by the engineer. Quite a contrary situation prevails in data processing.

The observation noted above does not apply, of course, to those aspects of data processing concerned with the construction of the hardware. The design and development of computing machinery proceeds along conventional engineering lines, very advanced engineering to be sure, but not different in kind from other modern engineering practice. The difficulty arises in the construction of software, the computer programs that must be prepared to make the machinery solve designated problems. In today's world, computer programming is a craft, not an engineering discipline, and it suffers from all the ills of lack of discipline. This is a consequence of the absence of an underlying fundamental science of the subject.

It is true that many universities have curricula entitled Computer Sciences and there is a growing body of theoretical developments upon which such curricula are based. While in no way do we mean to deprecate these activities, they are still far from adequate. Three problems exist. First, the coupling between the extant basic theories and applied practice is loose at best and, in many instances, nonexistent. This is a result of the lack of maturity of the subject and creates a situation analogous to that of a physicist being presented with the predicate calculus and some selected bits of set theory when what he requires is an ability to cope with nonlinear, partial differential equations.

The second problem is the lack of general agreement on questions of approach to fundamental problems. Here again the infancy of the subject is responsible. As an example, there are numerous techniques for describing the semantics of programming languages, most of which have been under formulation for over ten years (Steel 1966). Much still remains to be done in the fundamental area of determining the equivalence or lack thereof among these different descriptive methodologies. The situation is similar to that of metamathematics in the 1930's. The research problems available provide an exciting vista but hardly a stable platform upon which to base an undergraduate curriculum with an eye toward engineering application.

The third problem is that the theoretical base is only partial. In some areas there do not even exist contending theories. Clearly, until this situation is remedied, it will not be possible to construct the larger synthesis necessary to the establishment of a sound basis for an engineering discipline in data processing. We contend, and will argue below, that erotetic logic is a significant component of this missing basis.

A major and growing area of data processing applications is the data base management system (Jardine 1974). More than half of the growth in data processing described above will come from the installation of such systems. An integrated data base management system is a complex of computing machinery and computer programs whose purpose is to store a collection of data, some fixed and some volatile, and to provide on command retrieval and modification of requested data. These systems are large and complex. Great care must be taken in their design and implementation to insure that they behave in the intended fashion. An example of such a system is the airlines' reservation system.

Among the principal application areas for which an integrated data-base management system is useful is the inquiry system. Inquiry systems permit one or more individuals to ask questions of a data base whose collection of data represents a model of the world of interest. The system is expected to supply answers to the questions. The importance of a clear understanding of the question-answer relationship to the task of designing such systems is apparent. Very complex computer programs, expensive to develop and costly to operate, are a necessary ingredient of inquiry systems, and any analysis that provides insight and guidance for the design process, resulting in improved functioning and reduction of the attendant costs, is highly desirable.

Additionally, in many situations the inquiry stations attached to such systems are physically remote from the central computer hardware and, therefore, require electronic communication links which, as every telephone user knows, can be quite expensive. Erotetic logic has the capability of clarifying the question-answer relationship in such a way as to produce more efficient questioners, in the sense that the questioner can obtain the information he really wants with fewer inquiries. Minimization of the number of inquiries and necessary responses will result in more efficient, and thus less expensive, communications.

We emphasize here that inquiry systems do not depend on resolution of the problem of the reduction of natural language questions to some formal system. This is an exceedingly difficult problem, particularly when it is intended that the reduction be performed automatically. None of the presently installed inquiry systems in practical use outside of laboratories attempts such a reduction. There are a number of stylized, formal languages that are used for inquiry against data bases, and some of these pretend to be natural languages through the device of using severely limited vocabularies and highly constrained syntax. Nevertheless, they are, or at least are intended to be, strict formalism with unambiguous syntax and semantics. Given this situation, an erotetic logic formulated around formal languages serves adequately to represent the real situation. We do not deny the desirability of developments in the mapping of natural to formal language, but we do not see this as an essential link in applying erotetic logic as we develop it to the practical problems of analyzing inquiry systems.

Currently available inquiry languages are generally unsatisfactory in that they tend to be quite limited in the complexity of query that they permit. Typically, the extent of complexity allowed is that obtainable from finite composition of the connectives of the propositional calculus, together with their counterparts in the algebra of sets. The use of quantifiers in inquiry systems is sporadic at best and is generally incomplete and incoherent. An adequate development of erotetic logic would, we believe, make possible the design and implementation of inquiry languages and systems with far more power and utility than any available today.

Recent research has resulted in the development of a generalized architectural description of data-base management systems, making it possible to note with some reasonable precision the points of interface between queries and other aspects of the data-base management system (Steel 1975). This same work speaks as well to the character of the underlying assertoric logic and other properties of relevant erotetic logic. What we have essayed here is compatible with these data-processing developments. We are encouraged that the abyss between formal developments and ad hoc practice appears to be closing with some rapidity.

It is difficult to provide an accurate assessment of the potential for improvement through the mechanisms discussed above. Informal discussions with experts in the design and implementation of data base systems and inquiry languages lead us to believe that there is a reasonable likelihood of obtaining a factor-of-two improvement in the utility of inquiry languages and at least that much, quite likely more, in the efficiency of communicating, analyzing, and processing queries. These two effects compound multiplicatively, so we conclude that there is a potential for improvement of inquiry systems by at least a factor of four. This gain in effectiveness translates directly into cost savings. In view of the magnitude of the applications involved, the resulting savings can be measured in billions of dollars.

Before becoming too sanguine about this conclusion, however, we must note that much of this enhanced effectiveness could come about by the usual, far less formal, tuning, fiddling, and serendipity that is characteristic of most data-processing system development. For, while it is true that computer programming is a craft rather than a science, many of its practitioners are quite adept. Nevertheless, the development of a formal erotetic logic has the promise of substantial benefits.

In the interest of accurate historical representation, we must report that at the time these investigations began (1961) we were hardly prescient enough to anticipate the magnitude of growth of data base management system applications and their concomitant inquiry systems. We were aware simply of some then new and interesting experiments that were being conducted in various laboratories in the use of computers as question-answering devices. Nobody at that time foresaw the proliferation of massive integrated data-base management systems that is now fact. It was the case, however, that interest in the man-machine, question-answer interaction problem was a major motivating factor in stimulating this research.

The growth and proliferation of data base systems, especially those with many, widely scattered access terminals for inquiry, has created a new and monstrous problem, privacy of information. Heretofore, the privacy of collected data about an individual has been maintained, imperfectly to be sure, but rather effectively by the sheer magnitude of the task of retrieving the data from widely scattered and inconsistent files. With the development of integrated data-base management systems using high speed automatic computing machinery, it becomes feasible, and for certain purposes desirable, to develop dossier files on individuals. The possibilities for misuse of such files are legion. This problem is currently under wide but generally uninformed discussion in various public forums, including many legislative bodies, and, most recently, the Privacy Protection Study Commission established by Public Law 93–579 of December 31 1974. Some of the possibilities and dangers have recently been documented in a report of the Project on Computer Databanks of the National Academy of Sciences (Westin and Baker 1972). As we will discuss below, we believe the development of erotetic logic can contribute in a fundamental way to the search for acceptable solutions to this problem. Again, in candor, this essentially sociological motivation was not among our original concerns, but it is most assuredly a strong factor in our feeling a continuing need for development of the subject.

The fundamental problem of privacy in record keeping is hardly new. As we have noted, it is the element of the new technology that has heightened the urgency of dealing with the problem of privacy. Technology has nearly reached the stage where it will permit the collection of so much data about individuals into systems with such easy access that, in the absence of precautions, almost anyone could obtain virtually all recorded information about anyone else. This assertion is, in practice, an exaggeration because certain limits are already in place and can be maintained, for example, it is not necessary to combine existing files. However, present protective techniques, some of which are nearing the point of being imbedded in statutes, are generally unsatisfactory in that they tend to protect more than it is socially desirable to protect. For example, the statutory divorcement of social security records from internal revenue records has the virtue of preventing social security employees from obtaining income tax data on individuals, to which they have no right, but this protection technique also prohibits demographic studies of certain kinds that would be useful for various planning purposes and do no violence to anyone's individual rights. The situation is perhaps parallel to the use of a hacksaw where a scalpel is more appropriate.

Let us emphasize that privacy per se is an ethical and legal problem. It is not the prerogative of the logician or data-processing specialist to determine what should be private, excepting in his capacity as a concerned citizen. What is in the specialist's province is the development and explanation of the technology necessary to insure that what is supposed to be private remains so, and that what is supposed to be in the public domain is available. We see a significant role for erotetic logic to play in the development of such a technology.

The total complex of technology involved in the maintenance of privacy in data-base management systems is wide ranging (Martin 1973). It includes cryptographic techniques to insure the security of communications, applied psychology for avoidance of disgruntled employees, metallurgy in the design of tamper-proof safes and so on. Much of this has to do with the problem of preventing unwanted access to the data base. Perhaps the most difficult problem in this area is that of preventing the individual who has legitimate access to the data base for certain purposes from either deliberately or unwittingly obtaining information to which he should not have access. A formal erotetic logic permits an analysis of queries where what is and is not derivable from the answers to a set of questions is susceptible of formal proof. In this way it may be possible to develop algorithms that permit legitimate information to be provided that would necessarily be unavailable using current methods, just because the information might result in a loss of privacy. While it is not clear at present exactly how far a developed erotetic logic will permit the system designer to go toward the ideal of maintaining complete privacy while restricting nothing public, it is apparent that such developments are necessary to maximizing the possibilities.

We have examined the practical aspects of our motivation in somewhat more depth than is customary in such an essay as the present one for two reasons. First, some choices of procedure and notation, arbitrary from the purely logical point of view, have been made with these practicalities in mind. Indeed, it is probably the case that some choices we believe to have been made arbitrarily were unconsciously affected by the motivational bias. Secondly, while the formal developments are constructed for a possibly infinite universe, in any data processing application the universe (data base) is necessarily finite. Many complexities and undecidabilities fall away in the finite situation, of course, and we urge the reader interested in the practical applications discussed above to keep this in mind. We did not attempt in the above exposition to treat explicitly the special case that applies to the data-processing situation.

List of Numbered Displays

(1)   *What is the freezing point of water, in degrees Fahrenheit, under standard conditions?*

(2)   *Is glass a liquid at 70°F.?*

(3)   *Glass is a liquid at 70°F.*

(4)   *Tobacco smoking: a vice, a virtue, a vagary, an extravagance, a cure for all ills?*

(5) $\{A_1, \ldots, A_n\}$

(6) $(A_1, \ldots, A_n)$

(7) $?\rho(A_1, \ldots, A_n)$

(8)   *Has John stopped beating his wife?*

(9)   *Which positive integer is the smallest prime greater than 45?*

(10) *x is the smallest prime greater than 45.*

(11) *x is a positive integer.*

(12) *Which boys are brothers of which girls?*

(13) *x is a brother of y.*

(14) *x is a boy, and y is a girl.*

(15) *What is the solution of $a + x = b$?*

(16) $\langle X, g, Ax_1 \ldots x_n \rangle$

(17) $(C_1 x_1, \ldots, C_r x_r, x_{r+1}, \ldots, x_n \, // \, Ax_1 \ldots x_n)$

(18) $?\rho(C_1 x_1, \ldots, C_r x_r, x_{r+1}, \ldots, x_n \, // \, Ax_1 \ldots x_n)$

(19) $?\rho(x_1, \ldots, x_n \, // \, Ax_1 \ldots x_n)$

(20) *What is the positive square root of π?*

(21) $x > 0 \,\&\, \exists y(y$ is an integer $\&\, x = y \times 10^{-5})$
      $// \, x^2 \leqslant \pi < (x + 10^{-5})^2$

(22) *Which primes lie between 10 and 20?*

(23) $(x$ is an integer $// \, x$ is a prime between 10 and 20$)$.

(24) *13 alone is a prime lying between 10 and 20.*

(25) *13 and 17 alone are primes lying between 10 and 20.*

(26) *Which prime lies between 10 and 20?*

(27) *What's an example of a prime lying between 10 and 20?*

(28) *What are some of the primes lying between 10 and 20?*

(29) *Which primes lie between 10 and 20, or aren't there any?*

(29′) *What are the freezing points of water, in degrees Fahrenheit, under standard conditions?*

(30) $S \& C \& D, \ S \& C, \ S \& D, \ S$

(31) $S_1 \& \ldots \& S_p$

(32) $\{S_1, \ldots, S_p\}$

(33) $(S_1 \& \ldots \& S_p) \& C \& D$

(34) $(s \ c \ d)$

(35) $?(s \ c \ d)\sigma$

(36) $\binom{u}{v} \ c \ d)$

(37) $?\binom{u}{v} \ c \ d)\sigma.$

(38) *Did you say valor, or value?*

(39) *I said valor.*

(40) *I said value.*

(41) *I said valor, and I did not say value,*

(42) *11, 13, and 17.*

(43) *(11 is a prime between 10 and 20) & (13 is a prime between 10 and 20) & (17 is a prime between 20 and 20).*

(44) $S \& f(\sigma, S) \& D, \ or \ S \& f(\sigma, S)$

(45) $S \& Max(\sigma, S) \& D, \ or \ S \& Max(\sigma, S)$

(46) $\bar{B}_1 \& \ldots \& \bar{B}_r$

(47) *Which of lamb, beef, veal, and ham is on sale today?*

(48) (L, B, V, H)

(49) $Aa_{1_1} \ldots a_{1_n} \& \ldots \& Aa_{p_1} \ldots a_{p_n}$

(50) $\forall x_1 \ldots \forall x_n [C_1 x_1 \& \ldots \& C_r x_r \supset [Ax_1 \ldots x_n \supset$
$[(x_{1,n} = a_{1_{1,n}}) \lor \ldots \lor (x_{1,n} = a_{p_{1,n}})]]]$

(51) $(x \text{ is an integer} \,//\, P(x)).$

(52) $\forall x[x \text{ is an integer} \supset [P(x) \supset [(x = 11)\lor(x = 13)$
$\lor(x = 17)]]]$

(53) $?(s - d)\sigma$

(54) $?(s \,\forall\, d)\sigma$

(55) *Which of the kitchen, the pantry and the wine cellar
seems to you as likely a place as any to commence
looking for the missing hat pin?*

(56) *Was her ladyship wearing the emerald necklace, the
diamond bracelet, or both?*

(57) *Was it suicide or murder?*

(58) *What's at least one example of a truth among the
following: the butler is concealing something, the
upstairs maid knows more than she's telling, it would
be worth questioning the gardener once again?*

(59) *Who were the denouncers of Cataline?*

(60) $?(_1^- \,\forall\, d)$ *(x is a person // x is a denouncer of Cataline).*

(61) *Cicero and Tully*

(62) *2, 3, 5, 7, and VII*

(63) *What are at least five examples of primes?,*

(64) $?(_5^- - d)$ *(x is an integer // x is a prime)*

(65) $\&_{(1 \leqslant i < j \leqslant p)} \, \bigvee_{(1 \leqslant k \leqslant n)} (a_{i_k} \neq a_{j_k})$

(66) *Cicero is a denouncer of Cataline & Tully is a
denouncer of Cataline.*

(67) $?(s \, c \, -)\sigma$

(68) $?(s \, c \neq)\sigma$

(69) $?(_1^- \,\forall\, \neq)$ *(x is a person // x is a denouncer of Cataline)*

(70) *What are the square roots of 1/4?*

(71) $?(^-_1 \ \forall \neq)$ (x is rational $// x^2 = 1/4$)

(72) $((+1/2)^2 = +1/4) \ \& \ ((+2/4)^2 = +1/4) \ \& \ ((-1/2)^2$
      $= +1/4)$.

(73) $?(^1_1 \ -\,-)$ $(x \ // \ Fx)$

(74) $?(^1_1 \ -\,-)$ $(Cx \ // \ Fx)$

(75) $?(^-_1 \ -\,-)$ $(x \ // \ Fx)$

(76) *Which numbers are prime?*

(77) *What color is Tom?*

(78) $Des(Hx \ // \ b)$

(79) $\forall x(Ax \supset (Bx \equiv (Cx \lor Dx)))$

(80) x(No Ax are Bx except $C_1 x$, or ... or $C_n x$)

(81) $?^1 Why(x \ // \ Bx, c)$

(82) *I have never been married. _____*
      I was first married on _____.

(83) *If there are no more than five pairs of twin primes,*
      which are they, or if there are more than five such,
      what are at least six examples?

(84) *If you were to go, would you take an umbrella?*

(85) *If you are going, are you taking an umbrella?*

(86) *If you had a million dollars, on what would you be*
      spending it?

(87) *If you have a million dollars, on what are you spend-*
      ing it?

(88) *If you acquire a million dollars, on what will you*
      spend it?

(89) *Given that you are going, are you taking an umbrella?*

(90) *Given that John used to beat his present wife, has he*
      a wife whom he used to beat and has now stopped
      beating?

(91) $((S\&\overline{M} \lor \overline{S}\&M) \ / \ ?^1 \forall(S, M))$

(92) $(A \ /?^1 (A)) \cup (B \ /?^1 (B))$

(93) $?^1 (A, B)$

(94) $(A\ /?^1(A))\&(B\ /?^1(B))$

(95) $?\forall(A, B)$

(96)   *Is the present king of France bald?*

(97)   *What is the width of the desk?*

(98)   *How fast did Jones drive down Main Street last night?*

(99)   *How many bones in a lion?*

(100) $?^1(A\lor B,\ C\&D)$

Bibliography of the Theory of Questions and Answers, by Urs Egli and Hubert Schleichert

Compiled by Urs Egli and Hubert Schleichert

Introductory Remarks This bibliography is in four parts, as follows: A. Logic and philosophy of language; B. Linguistics; C. Automatic question-answering; D. Psychology and pedagogy. With respect to citations from the text, nearly all are to part A, except those from chapter 4, which are all to part C.

The preparation of a bibliography of logical, linguistic, and other works on questions and answers was begun independently by both of us some years ago. Late in the summer of 1975 we decided to join forces, which resulted in the present bibliography. We have sought to be as complete as possible, especially in the section devoted to philosophical treatments of the topic, but we are aware of the fact that there exist works not listed in the bibliography. As we intend to complete the list and to keep it up to date, we hereby offer a printout of the most updated version to everyone who will send us offprints of relevant articles or will help us otherwise. (The list is computer maintained, which accounts for the absence of some diacritical marks.) A preliminary version of this bibliography appeared in *Linguistische Berichte* 41, 1976, 105-128.

For some of the articles and books abstracts are given, while others are left with no annotation. The selection of those items which have been abstracted does not reflect any theoretical principle. Abstracts are given whenever the author himself provided one, or when we had the time to do it. So whether an abstract is given or not does not indicate anything as to the quality of a paper; it is largely a matter of accident.

We wish to thank the many colleagues who helped us in the preparation of the bibliography. Special thanks are due to Gerlinde Sterba and Heribert Ficht, who did a lot of the "dirty" job of typing, checking, and unifying the material.

This work has been supported by the Deutsche Forschungsgemein-

schaft (DFG) as a part of the "Sonderforschungsbereich Linguistik"
(SFB 99).
University of Konstanz
Sonderforschungsbereich 99
D-7750 Konstanz, Germany

List of Abbreviations

ACM   Association for Computing Machinery
AFIPS   American Federation of Information Processing Societies
Comm.   Communications of the
J.   Journal of (the)
JSL   Journal of symbolic logic
Phil.   Philosophy
Proc.   Proceedings of the

A. Logic and Philosophy of Language

Ajdukiewicz, K. (1926). "Analiza semantyczna zdania pytainego"
    (Semantic analysis of the structure of questions). *Ruch filozoficzny*
    10, 194–195.
—— (1934). *Logiczne podstawy nauczania* (Logical foundations of
    teaching). Warsaw.
—— (1974). *Pragmatic logic.* Reidel, Dordrecht, Netherlands

    Chapter 6 "Questions and interrogative sentences"
Anderson, A. R., and Belnap, N. D., Jr. (1975). *Entailment: the logic
    of relevance and necessity,* vol. 1. Princeton University Press,
    Princeton. 542 pp.

    This item is cited in the text, but it is not directly on questions.

Apostel, L. (1969). "A proposal in the analysis of questions." *Logique
    et analyse* 12, 376–381.

    If X asks Y whether p is true, then X presupposes the following:
    (1) X does not know whether p or non p; (2) X believes that Y
    should know whether p; (3) X believes that the addressee Y should
    assert p resp. non p; (4) X believes that it is possible for Y to do so.
    By means of these modal notions a definition of "presupposition of
    question q" is achieved.

Åqvist, L. (1965). *A new approach to the logical theory of interrogatives.* Almqvist & Wiksell, Uppsala. 174 pp. Published again as *A new approach to the logical theory of interrogatives: analysis and formalization.* Tuebinger Beitraege zur Linguistik 65, Verlag Gunter Narr, Tuebingen, 1975.

Contents: Introduction; Logical machinery; Questions and their classification; Questions formalizable within the framework of PIE; Questions requiring formalization within the framework of QIE; Interrogative presupposition and truth; The problem of direct answers. (PIE = propositional imperative-epistemic logic; QIE = quantified imperative-epistemic logic.)

(Review by C. L. Hamblin: *Australasian j. phil.* 44, 1966, 385–390.)

(Review by David Harrah: *JSL* 32, 1967, 403–404.)

—— (1967). "Semantic and pragmatic characterizability of linguistic usage." *Synthese* 17, 281–291.

—— (1969). "Scattered topics in interrogative logic." In: Davis, Hockney, Wilson (eds.), *Philosophical logic,* 2d ed., pp. 114–121. Reidel, Dordrecht, Netherlands.

—— (1971). "Revised foundations for imperative epistemic and interrogative logic." *Theoria* 37, 33–73.

—— (1972). "On the analysis and logic of questions." In: R. E. Olson and A. M. Paul (eds.), *Contemporary philosophy in Scandinavia,* pp. 27–39. Johns Hopkins University Press, Baltimore and London.

Aristotle. *De interpretatione*: 20b.

——. *Topica*:103b, 104a, 155b–158a.

Bastian, H. (1969). *Theologie der Frage.* Munich.

Bell, M. (1975). "Questioning." *Philosophical Quarterly* 25, 193–212.

Belnap, N. D., Jr. (1963). *An analysis of questions; preliminary report.* Technical memorandum 7 1287 1000/00, System Development Corp., Santa Monica, Calif. 160 pp.

(Review by C. L. Hamblin: *Australasian j. phil.* 42, 1964, 146–151.)

(Review by David Harrah: *JSL* 37, 1972, 420–421.)

—— (1966). "Questions, answers, and presuppositions." *J. phil.* 63, 609-611.

Discussion of Bromberger 1966-a. Suggestion to formulate Bromberger's explanation of the answer to "Why is t a B" syntactically. Accordingly an answer should consist of the following four parts: (1) an "abnormic law," something like "no As are Bs, except C_1s and C_2s"; (2) an explicit statement of the required extrasyntactic conditions on abnormic laws; (3) the sentence "t is an A"; (4) the explanation that t is a C_1, resp. t is a C_2.

(Review by M. J. Cresswell: *JSL* 33, 1968, 310.)

—— (1969-a) "Åqvist's corrections-accumulating question sequences." In: Davis, Hockney, Wilson, (eds.), *Philosophical logic,* 2d ed. pp. 122-134. Reidel, Dordrecht, Netherlands.

—— (1969-b). "Questions, their presuppositions and how they can fail to arise." In: K. Lambert (ed.), *The logical way of doing things,* pp. 23-37. Yale University Press, New Haven.

A question Q presupposes a sentence B iff the truth of B is a logically necessary condition for there being some true answer to Q, i.e. iff every true answer to Q logically implies the sentence B. "Has John stopped beating his wife?" presupposes that John used to beat his wife. "Is the present king of France bald?" presupposes that there is now a king of France. Most questions have several presuppositions, but some questions have no substantive presuppositions, such as "Are there any unicorns?" These questions are "safe," all others are "risky." Normally the questioner is responsible for the truth of the presupposition. To this extent questions often convey information, e.g. "Do you know whom your wife kissed?" The definition of "presupposition" in the second wording above is independent of interpreting the examples in Russell's or Strawson's way. A question Q is relevant to a set of questions P relative to a set of sentences S, iff a (positive or negative) answer implies (together with S) some answer to some member of P.

—— (1972). "S-P interrogatives." *J. philosophical logic* 1, 331-346.

Bolzano, B. (1837). *Wissenschaftslehre.* Scientia Verlag, Aalen, W. Germany, 1970.

Questions are treated in paragraphs 145 and 163.

Bromberger, S. (1966-a). "Questions." *J. phil.* 63, 597-606.

   (Review by M. J. Cresswell: *JSL* 33, 1968, 310.)

—— (1966-b). "Why-questions." In: R. Colodny (ed.), *Mind and cosmos,* pp. 86-111. Pittsburgh University Press, Pittsburgh. Also in: B. A. Brody (ed.), *Readings in the philosophy of science,* pp. 66-87. Prentice-Hall, Englewood Cliffs, New Jersey.

   This paper is discussed in Teller 1974.

Bunge, M. (1967). *Scientific research I.* Springer, Berlin.

   Chapter 4.2 (pp. 170-183) deals with questions.

Cackowski, Z. (1966). *Problemy i pseudoproblemy* (Problems and pseudo problems). Warsaw.

Carnap, R. (1928). *Scheinprobleme in der Philosophie.* Suhrkamp, Frankfurt, 1966.

—— (1934). *Die logische Syntax der Sprache.* Springer, Vienna. English edition: *The logical syntax of language.* Routledge and Kegan Paul, London, 1967.

   Remarks on questions in paragraph 76, the last two sections.

Castelli, E. (ed.) (1968). *Il problema della domanda.* Archivio di Filosofia, CEDAM, Padua, Italy.

   Contents: E. Castelli, Premessa; E. Paci, Domanda, risposta e significato; G. Semerari, Del domandare; V. Somenzi, La domanda assurda—può il cervello pensare; G. Calogero, Intorno al problema della "domanda"; E. Agazzi, Logica e domanda; M. Laeng, Educazione alla domanda; G. Derossi, La struttura dell'interrogazione; M. Olivetti, L'istanza critica nella domanda ontologica; S. Piro, La domanda dello schizofrenico; M. Olivetti, La domanda sul futuro del christianesimo; A. Cortese, La domanda su Kierkegaard.

Church, A. (1956). *Introduction to mathematical logic,* vol. 1. Princeton University Press, Princeton. 378 pp.

   This item is cited in the text, but it is not directly on questions.

Cohen, F. S. (1929). "What is a question." *The monist* 39, 350-364.

Collingwood, R. G. (1939). *An autobiography.* Oxford University Press, Oxford.

There is a chapter on questions and answers.

—— (1940). *An essay on metaphysics.* Oxford University Press, Oxford.

Cresswell, M. J. (1965-a). "On the logic of incomplete answers." *JSL* 30, 65–68.

Let "$\mathbf{Si}p(Q\ b)A(b)$" mean: "p is an incomplete answer to the question, Which b are A?" Let "f" be a variable for functions of propositional arguments like "it is not the case that . . . , "it is logically possible that . . . , " etc. Then the notion of an incomplete answer can be defined by $\mathbf{Si}p(Q\ b)\ A(b)$ = (by definition) $p\ \&\ (f)\ (((b)fA(b)\ \&\ (q)(r)\ ((fq\ \&\ fr)\supset f(q\ \&\ r)))\supset fp)$. Using this definition one can prove that (1) any true statement $A(b)$ counts as an incomplete answer, and (2) the conjunction of any two answers to a question is itself an answer to that question. An $\mathbf{Si}$ answer, however, can sometimes be a complete answer. (See also Cresswell 1965-b, and Kubinski 1967).

(Review by Gerold Stahl: *JSL* 31, 1966, 498.)

—— (1965-b). "The logic of interrogatives." In: J. Crossley and M. Dummett (eds.), *Formal systems and recursive functions,* pp. 8–11. North-Holland, Amsterdam.

Description of a method how to define in a modal system the concept "*Spd*" meaning "*p* is the answer to *d*?" For *S* the following laws hold: (1) $(Spd\ \&\ Sqd)\supset(p=q)$; (2) $(\exists p)Spd$, (every question has an answer); (3) $Spd\supset p$; (4) $\square\ (p\equiv q)\ \&\ Spd\supset Sqd$ (here "$\square$" means "necessarily"). Identity of two questions, *d, e* is defined as $(p)\ \square\ (Spd\equiv Spe)$. Let "$(Qb)A(b)?$" mean "For which b's does A hold?"; the answer to this question will be the true conjunction of all $A(b_i)$'s or $\sim A(b_i)$'s for every b_i. A formalization of this concept is given.

(Review by Gerold Stahl: *JSL* 31, 1966, 668.)

Fair, F. K. (1971). *The logic of some which- and whether-questions.* Ph.D. diss., University of Georgia. University Microfilms, Ann Arbor, Mich., 1972.

—— (1973). "The fallacy of many questions; or, how to stop beating your wife." *Southwestern j. phil.* 4, 89-92.

Finkeldei, H.-J. (1954). *"Grund und Wesen der Fragens."* Diss. phil., Heidelberg.

Frege, G. (1919). "Die Verneinung: eine logische Untersuchung." In: G. Patzig (ed.), *G. Frege: Logische Untersuchungen,* pp. 54-71. Vandenhoeck und Ruprecht, Goettingen, W. Germany, 1966.

Freudenthal, H. (1960). *LINCOS: design of a language for cosmic intercourse, part 1.* North-Holland, Amsterdam.

Formalization of questions in chap. 3.

Gasking, D. A. T. (1946). "Types of questions." *Melbourne University Magazine,* pp. 4-6.

Giedymin, J. (1964). *Problemy, Zalozenia, Rozstrzygnięcia.* Studia nad logicznymi podstawami nauk spolecznych (Problems, suppositions, solutions, studies on the logical foundations of the social sciences). Poznań, Poland.

Hamblin, C. L. (1958). "Questions." *Australian j. phil.* 36, 159-168.

The question "Is Smith at home?" has been equated with "I don't know whether he is at home and would like to know it." In doing so the question itself is not reduced, but its attendant circumstances are described. The assertion *"p"* is not the same as "I think that *p*." Hamblin postulates (1) the answer to a question is a sentence; (2) when you know what counts as an admissible answer you have understood the question; (3) the possible answers are a set of mutually exclusive possibilities. A calculus of questions might be developed, analogous to common logic.

(Review by David Harrah: *JSL* 28, 1963, 258.)

—— (1963). "Questions aren't statements." *Phil. of science* 30, 62-63.

Short discussion of Harrah 1961 and Leonard 1959 and 1961. Questions are not equivalent with their answers. Leonard asserts that a disjunctive question is a true sentence of the form *"A or B"* (exclusive or). Here the expression "disjunction" is ambiguous. In a question it is about the possibility of selection for the answer, but in an assertion reality is described. The equation of questions and answers leads to absurd consequences.

(Review by Gerold Stahl: *JSL* 31, 1966, 666–668.)

—— (1967). "Question." In: Paul Edwards (ed.), *The encyclopedia of philosophy,* pp. 49–53. Macmillan and Free Press, New York.
—— (1971). "Mathematical models of dialogue." *Theoria* 37, 130–155.
—— (1973). "Questions in Montague English." *Foundations of language* 10, 41–53.

This paper is discussed by Egli 1976.

Harrah, D. (1961). "A logic of questions and answers." *Phil. of science* 28, 40–46.

A logic of questions and answers already exists within the logic of statements, if we identify "whether"-questions with true exclusive disjunctions and "which"-questions with true existential quantifications. Being true statements, questions cannot presuppose false assumptions and cannot be meaningless. The question-and-answer process is interpreted as an information-matching game. Complete and partial answers can be distinguished and various relations of relevance, independence, and resolution defined.

(Review by N. D. Belnap, Jr.: *JSL* 29, 1964, 136–138.)

—— (1963). *Communication: a logical model.* MIT Press, Cambridge, Mass., 105 pp.

Contents: Aim of this book; Tools we shall use; Message effect; The receiver's language; The receiver's logic; Theory of questions; Logic of questions; Logic of answers; Question sets; Adequacy of our theory; Information; Communication events; Message-processing; News-value; Meaning; Message adequacy.

(Review by N. D. Belnap, Jr.: *JSL* 29, 1964, 136–138.)

(Review by C. L. Hamblin: *Australasian j. phil.* 42, 1964, 146–151.)

(Review by J. Giedymin: *Studia logica* 15, 1964, 304–308.)

—— (1966). "Question generators." *J. phil.* 63, 606–608.

(Review by M. J. Cresswell: *JSL* 33, 1968, 310.)

—— (1969-a). "Erotetic logistics." In: K. Lambert (ed.), *The logical way of doing things,* pp. 3–21. Yale University Press, New Haven.

The central notions are those of interest, interest-expression-system, and interest-contract. An interest is represented as a set consisting of the area of interest, the things that satisfy the interest, and the things that partially satisfy the interest. Knowing the latter two is knowing the interest. The central item in an interest-expression-system is the set of interest-expression-functions which assigns sequences of expressions (of a given language) to interests. These sequences are said to express the interest. Questions are able and mostly used to express interests. An interest-contract consists of an interest, a set of commitments for both questioner and respondent, and a function which assigns payments to the responses. In a fair contract, the set of commitments includes all presuppositions of a question.

—— (1969-b). "On completeness in the logic of questions." *American philosophical quarterly* 6, 158–164.

Harrah gives five fields of possible investigations in the logic of questions: articulation, consistency, effectiveness, completeness, and coherence. He works out one completeness property and shows by a diagonal method that, if direct answer is to be constructive, one must choose between constructivity of questions and completeness in the sense that to each set of sentences there is a question such that this set is the set of its direct answers. He develops a theory of interest very much the same as in Harrah 1969-a.

—— (1975)."A system for erotetic sentences." In: Anderson, Marcus, Martin (eds.), *The logical enterprise,* pp. 235–245. Yale University Press, New Haven.
—— (1976). "Formal message theory and non-formal discourse." In: T. A. Van Dijk (ed.), *Pragmatics of language and literature,* pp. 59–76. North-Holland, Amsterdam.
Heinrich, K. (1953). *Versuch ueber das Fragen und die Frage.* Diss. phil., Freie Universitaet, Berlin.
Hintikka, J. (1974). "Questions about questions." In: M. K. Munitz and P. K. Unger (eds.), *Semantics and philosophy,* pp. 103–158. New York University Press, New York.

—— (1975). "Answers to questions." In: J. Hintikka: *The intentions of intentionality and other new models for modalities*, pp. 137–158. Reidel, Dordrecht, Netherlands.

—— (1976-a). "The semantics of questions and the questions of semantics." *Acta Philosophica Fennica* 28, 4. Helsinki, Finland.

—— (1976-b). "The question of ?: a comment on Urs Egli." *Dialectica* 3.

—— (forthcoming). "Multiple questions and the presuppositions of linguistic semantics."

Hiż, H. (1962). "Questions and answers." *J. phil.* 59, 253–265.

A question can be obtained from a sentence by replacing a phrase in it by a variable and prefixing a "questioner." Thus it consists of two parts, a questioner and the datum questionis. From a datum questionis an answer is obtainable by replacing the free variables by a phrase of the proper syntactical category. Some, but not all categories can easily be questioned in English: "For what x, John read x to Peter?" gives "What did John read to Peter?"; "For what x, John x the book to Peter?" gives "What did John do with the book to Peter?"; starting from "By noise John means the music" one gets "For what x, by noise John x the music?", which can be expressed in natural English only in a complicated way. Generally it is easy to question nouns as e.g. in "Who read the book?" Questions concerning adjectives are more complicated and one has to use "interrogative proadjectival phrases," e.g. "What kind of music do you like?"; "What sort of books . . . ?" The question "Was it before or after the concert that you slept?" may be answered by "During the concert." So "before or after" is an indication of the category of answer we want (i.e. a preposition). A composite sentence like "If the state is just, the people are unhappy" has to be questioned using a circumlocution: "Is it the case that if the state . . . ?" When one speaks about relations between sentences, nominalizations are still more frequent: "For what x, the state is just x the people are unhappy?" gives "What relation holds between the justice of the state and the unhappiness of the people?" The "conceptual" question "What is a palimpsest?" is of a complicated form, roughly as follows: "For what p, p is a true sentence and every true sentence containing the word 'palimpsest' is inferable from p . . . ?" Answers to conceptual questions are not restricted in their form, but they can never be complete.

(Review by David Harrah: *JSL* 32, 1967, 547–548.)

Hurrell, P. (1964). "Interrogatives, testability and truth-value." *Phil. of science* 31, 173–182.

A discussion of Leonard 1959 and 1961, and Wheatley 1961 concerning assigning truth-values to interrogatives.

Ingarden, R. (1925). "Essentiale Fragen, ein Beitrag zu dem Wesens-problem." *Jahrbuch fuer Philosophie und phaenomenologische Forschung,* vol. 7, pp. 125–304. Halle, E. Germany.

Contents: Die Frage ueberhaupt und ihre Eigenschaften; Scheidung verwandter Bedeutungen der essentialen Fragen; Eindeutige Bestimmung, Erkenntnis des Wesens und Klassifikation des Gegenstandes; Ontologische Grundlagen der Bestimmungsurteile; Das Wesensurteil und seine ontologischen Grundlagen. Die reale Definition; Ob und in welchen Grenzen der Gegenstand der Erkenntnis von dem Erkenntnisakte bzw. Subjekte abhaengig ist?

Jungius, J. (1638). *Logica Hamburgensis.* Latin-German, Hamburg, 1957.

Questions are dealt with in book 5.

Kleiner, S. A. (1970). "Erotetic logic and the structure of scientific revolution." *British journal for the phil. of science* 21, 149–165.

Knight, T. S. (1966). "Questions and universals." *Phil. and phenomenological research* 27, 564–576.

Every "indirect" (= which) question specifies the class the wanted element belongs to and states the properties of the wanted element. "Who murdered B?" specifies the class of human beings and states the property of being B's murderer. The specification can be less precise, e.g. "Why did the TV set go off?" asks for a reason. When no class at all is specified, the question is no longer "inquisitive," e.g. "What exists?" or "What is beauty?" Questions arise out of an irritation, a striking situation. This presupposes that the questioner is familiar to a certain degree with the context, because without any knowledge you cannot be irritated, and therefore you cannot put any questions.

(Review by Gerold Stahl: *JSL* 33, 1968, 612–613.)

Kubinski, T. (1960). "An essay in the logic of questions." *Atti del XII. Congr. Intern. di Filosofia,* Firenze, vol. 5, p. 315.

This is an outline of a calculus for the logic of questions. Let "J" denote a set of expressions closed with respect to connectives and quantifiers. The set $J \cup P_1 \cup P_2$ is the "interrogative extension" of J. P_1 is the set of decision-questions; it is the smallest set such that: (1) if R belongs to J, then ?R belongs to P_1, and (2) if X, Y belong to P_1, then $X \vee^* Y$ and $X \&^* Y$ belong to P_1. ("$\vee^*$" resp. "$\&^*$" are to be read as "or" resp. "and"). P_2 is the smallest set such that (1) if $R(x_1 \ldots x_n)$ belongs to J, then $\langle x_1 \rangle \ldots \langle x_n \rangle R(x_1 \ldots x_n)$ belongs to P_2. ("$\langle x_2 \rangle$," etc. may be permuted in any manner.) (2) (As in (2) of definition of p_1.) p_2 is the set of "supplement questions." $\langle x_1 \rangle R(x_1)$ is to be read as "for which x_1 is $R(x_1)$?" Going backwards from a member Z of P_1 to a corresponding member of J, one gets the "root" of that question (denoted by "QZ"). E.g. $(P\&Q)\vee R$ is the root of $?(P\&Q) \vee^* ?R$. Let X, Y be subsets from J, let CnY be the class of all expressions derivable from Y, and K the set of all contradictory subsets of J. The notion CY ("C-derivation from Y") is then defined by: X is a subset of CY = (by definition) X is a subset of CnY and if Y is in K, then X is in K. The expression "$!+A \times B$"means "A is an affirmative answer to question B on ground of X": $!+A \times B$ = (by definition) QB is an element of $C(\{A\}\cup X)$, B is an element of P_1,X is a subset of J, A is an element of J. If one replaced here C-derivability by Cn, then any contradictory member of J would be an affirmative (and also a negative) answer to all decision-questions. Analogous definitions are given for supplement-questions. Finally, the concepts of equivalence of questions, dependency of questions, and the law of commutation for interrogative quantifiers $\langle x_1 x_2 \ldots \rangle$ are formulated.

(Review by David Harrah: *JSL* 28, 1963, 258–259.)

—— (1966). "Przeglad niektorych zagadnien logiki pytan" (A review of some problems of the logic of questions. Polish, with summaries in English and Russian). *Studia logica* 18, 105–137.

(Review by Pavel Materna: *JSL* 32, 1967, 548–549.)

—— (1967). "Some observations about a notion of incomplete answer." *Studia logica* 21, 39–42.

The definition of "incomplete answer" given in Cresswell 1965-b contains a general quantifier (f) binding a functorial variable f. Cresswell does not make completely precise the meaning of this quantifier (f). Now a wff of the form $(f)\Psi(f)$ is often regarded as an abbreviation of a finite conjunction of the form $\Psi(K_1)\&\ldots$ $\&\Psi(K_m), K_1,\ldots,K_m$ being a sequence of 1-argument sentential connectives. But under this interpretation of (f), Cresswell's definition of incomplete answer can be shown to be inadequate.

—— (1968). "The logic of questions." In: Raymond Klibansky (ed.), *Contemporary philosophy–La philosophie contemporaine I*, pp. 185–189. La Nuova Italia Editrice, Florence.

—— (1969). "Analiza logiczna pojecia zalozenia pytania" (A logical analysis of the notion of presupposition of questions). *Rozprawy filozoficzne. Towarzystwo naukowe w Toruniu. Prace wydzialu filologiczno-filozoficznego* 21, 189–200.

Two different categories of presuppositions of questions are defined, discussed, and compared.

—— (1970-a). "Pewne klasy relacji miedzy pytaniami" (Some classes of relations among questions). *Ruch filosoficzny* 28, 186–191.

Some finite classes of binary relations among questions are taken into account. Two different relations of the same class are exclusive, whereas the logical sum of all relations of the same class is a universal binary relation. A relation connects two questions P and Q if either some special relations connect the class of all direct answers to P and Q, or some relations connect some classes of presuppositions of some kind of the question P and Q.

—— (1970-b). *Wstep do logicznej teorii pytan* (Introduction to the logic of questions). Panstowe Wydawnictwo Naukowe, Warsaw. 118 pp.

Part 1 is devoted to various interrogative operators as well as various types of questions. Part 2 analyses some classes of binary relations among questions as well as some special notions of the theory of consequence which are useful in question logic. In part 3 some types of presuppositions of questions are discussed and, in addition, further relations among questions are investigated. Various approaches to the logic of questions, due mainly to Åqvist, Belnap, and Stahl, are presented, analysed, and compared in part 4.

—— (1973-a). "Woonaczanie klas pytan przez systemy algebraiczne" (Determining of classes of questions by algebraic systems). *Ruch filozoficzny* 31, 37–42.

A rather complicated semantic notion of determining a class of questions by an algebraic system is introduced. Many theorems of the paper answer the problem, Which classes of questions are determined by which algebraic systems (like finite free Boolean algebras).

—— (1973-b). "Twierdzenia o relacjach sprowadzalnosci operatorow pytajnych" (Theorems on reducibility of interrogative operators). *Ruch filozoficzny* 31, 213–220.

Some notions of reducibility of one interrogative operator to another are defined, deducibility being a special sort of definability adapted to question-logic. Many theorems characterize those notions and solve the problem of reducibility of various types of interrogative operators.

Leonard, H. (1959). "Interrogatives, imperatives, truth, falsity, and lies." *Phil. of science* 26, 172–186.

(Review by Gerold Stahl: *JSL* 31, 1966, 666–668.)

—— (1961). "A reply to Professor Wheatley." *Phil. of science* 28, 55–64.

—— (1967). *Principles of reasoning.* Dover Publications, New York. 620 pp.

Sections 3 and 4 are concerned with questions.

Llewelyn, J. (1964-a). "What is a question." *Australasian j. phil.* 42, 67–85.

A discussion of views of Wheatley, Mayo, Prior, Cohen. Questions are neither imperatives nor statements.

(Review by David Harrah: *JSL* 34, 1969, 644-645.)

—— (1964-b). "Propositions as answers." *American philosophical quarterly* 2, 305-311.

Loeser, F. (1968). *Interrogativlogik.* VEB Deutscher Verlag der Wissenschaften, Berlin. 106 pp.

Mackay, D. M. (1960). "What makes a question?" *The listener* 63, 789-790.

—— (1961). "The informational aspects of questions and commands." In: C. Cherry (ed.), *Information theory.* Papers read at a symposium on information theory held at the Royal Institution, London, August 29-September 2, 1960; pp. 469-476. Butterworths, London.

Mayo, B. (1956). "Deliberative questions: A criticism." *Analysis* 16, 58-63.

Comments on Wheatley 1955.

Minkowski, E. (1970). "Question, interrogation, problème." *Revue de métaphysique et morale* 75, 257-261.

Moritz, M. (1940). "Zur Logik der Frage." *Theoria* 6, 123-149.

(Review by Ernest Nagel: *JSL* 5, 1940, 159-160.)

Mostowski, A. (1957). "On a generalization of quantifiers." *Fundamenta mathematicae* 44, 12-36.

This item is cited in the text, but it is not directly on questions.

Moutafakis, N. J. (1975). "A new look at erotetic communication." *Notre Dame j. formal logic* 16, 217-228.

Orgass, R. J. (1970). *Logic and question answering.* IBM RC 3122 1970.

This is mainly a summary of Belnap's work.

Petrov, Ju. A. (1969). "Version of erotetic logic." *Proc. 14th International Congress of Phil.* III, Vienna, pp. 17-23.

Post, J. F. (1965). "A defense of Collingwood's theory of presuppositions." *Inquiry* 8, 332-354.

Presley, C. F. (1959). "A note on questions." *Australasian j. phil.* 37, 64-66.

Notes on Hamblin 1958.

(Review by David Harrah: *JSL* 28, 1963, 258.)

Prior, A. and Prior, M. (1955). "Erotetic logic." *Philosophical review* 64, 43–59.

The Priors discuss Whately's *Logic* (1826) and *Rhetoric* (1828) and take up two of his intentions: to extend the Kantian division of judgments in his "Prolegomena" to questions, and to reduce all questions to (pure) what-questions. The reduction is done by re-wording a yes/no question "*B*?" by "What is the truth-value of *B*?" and a (qualified) what-question like "What color is grass?" by "What is the color of grass?" As for Kant's division of judgments, the aspect of relation is discussed first. Categorical questions are yes/no questions. Hypothetical (conditional) questions are questions like "If you go out tonight, where do you go?" where an answer is expected only if the if-clause is true. A question is called disjunctive, iff it asks for one out of several alternatives, and the truth of exactly one alternative is presupposed. The distinctions subsumed under the aspect of quality (affirmative, negative, infinite) are not applicable to questions, but only to the relation between questions and answers. The same holds for the aspect of quantity (universal, particular, singular), which is involved in the fact that the same question may be answered with greater or less determinateness, and for modality (problematic, assertive, apodictic), which describes the possibility of answering "possibly," "I have not decided" or the like.

(Review by N. Rescher: *JSL* 20, 1955, 302.)

Reichenbach, H. (1947). *Elements of symbolic logic.* Free Press, New York.

Paragraph 57 contains remarks on interrogatives.

Rescher, N. (1967). "Avicenna on the logic of questions." *Archiv fuer Geschichte der Philosophie* 49, 1–6.

Ritchie, A. D. (1943). "The logic of question and answer." *Mind* 52, 24–38.

Discussion of some aspects of R. G. Collingwood's *Essay on metaphysics* (1940). This paper has no connection with the theory of interrogatives.

Rombach, H. (1952). "Ueber Ursprung und Wesen der Frage." In: *Symposion (Jahrbuch fuer Philosophie)*, vol. 3, pp. 135-236.

This paper is written in the tradition of the Heidegger school. Contents: Die Anfrage im Miteinandersein; Die Forschungsfrage an das seiende Selbst; Die Entscheidungsfrage ueber das Ganze des Daseins; Schluss.

Sabilin, V. (1961). "Das Problem der Frage und Antwort." *Filosofskie Nauki* 1.

Schlick, M. (1935). "Unanswerable questions?" *The philosopher*, vol. 13. Also in: M. Schlick, *Gesammelte Aufsaetze 1926-1936,* pp. 369-375. Gerold, Vienna, 1938.

—— (1936). "Meaning and verification." *Philosophical review* 45, 339-369. Also in: M. Schlick, *Gesammelte Aufsaetze 1926-1936,* pp. 336-367. Gerold, Vienna, 1938.

Segeth, W. (1966). "Erkenntnistheoretische Bemerkungen zum Begriff der Frage." In: Parthey, Vogel, and Waechter (eds.), *Problemstruktur und Problemverhalten in der wissenschaftlichen Forschung,* pp. 39-44. Rostocker philosophische Manuskripte, vol. 3. Rostock, E. Germany.

Sperantia, E. (1936). "Remarques sur la proposition interrogative: Projet d'une logique du problème." *Actes du congrès internationale de philosophie scientifique* 1935, Paris, vol. 7, pp. 18-28.

(Review by H. N. Castañeda: *JSL* 22, 1957, 93-94.)

Stadler, A. (1908). "Die Frage als Prinzip des Erkennens und die 'Einleitung' der Kritik der reinen Vernunft." *Kantstudien* 13, 238-248.

Stahl, G. (1956). "La logica de las preguntas." *Anales de la Universidad de Chile,* no. 102, 71-75.

(Review by Hector N. Castañeda: *JSL* 22, 1957, 93-94.)

—— (1961). "Preguntas y premisas." *Revista di filosofia,* no. 1, 3-9.

(Review by H. N. Castañeda: *JSL* 28, 1963, 257-258.)

—— (1962). "Fragenfolgen." In: M. Kaesbauer and F. Kutschera (eds.), *Logik und Logikkalkuel,* pp. 149, 157. Alber, Freiburg i. Br., W. Germany.

Questions are considered as classes of sufficient answers. Thus "identity of questions," "subquestion," "union of question," etc., can be defined. A question sequence (Fragenfolge) is e.g. "Does Smith know Australia? If he does not know it, who knows it?" The second question has to be answered only if the first cannot be answered. Question sequences have often the grammatical form of disjunctions, e.g. "Does Smith know Australia, or who else knows it?"

(Review by David Harrah: *JSL* 28, 1963, 259.)

—— (1963). "Un développement de la logique des questions." *Revue philosophique de la France et de l'étranger* 153, no. 3, 293–301.

(Review by David Harrah: *JSL* 32, 1967, 548.)

—— (1969). "The effectivity of questions." *Noûs* 3, 211–218.

Questions are considered as classes of sufficient answers. Let [*Hx*?] be an "individual question"; then *Ha, Hb, . . .* are "simple answers." Simple answers, which are not negations of theorems of the considered system, are called "direct answers." "Perfect answers" are defined as direct answers or negations of direct answers or conjunctions of such expressions, excluding negations of theorems. A "sufficient answer" is an expression which (1) implies at least one perfect answer that is not a theorem, or (2) is a theorem, and at least one perfect answer is a theorem. Thus the following expressions are all members of the class [*Hx*?] : *Ha, Ha&Hb,* $(x) \sim Hx$, *Q&Ha,* . . . . This definition may be changed by speaking of "conclusion from a premiss class *S*" in place of "theorem." Then the negations of conclusions from *S* are to be excluded. The definitions apply also for "functional questions" like $(f?A)$ ("What propositional functions are satisfied by *A*?"). Truth-questions like $(A \, f? \, B)$ or $(g?A)$ ask for two-place resp. one-place truth-functions which hold between *A* and *B,* resp. apply to *A.* (That is, yes-no-questions are considered as one-place truth-functional questions.) "Effectivity" of questions means: it is decidable whether a given expression is an answer to a given question. "Effective enumerability" of questions means: it is decidable whether a supposed formal justification for including an expression in a question (i.e., in the class of answers) is correct. Theorems: within a decidable system (1) the class of perfect answers of the individual-, functional- and truth-questions is effective; (2) any truth-question is effective; (3) any individual and functional question is effectively enumerable. However, in an undecidable system there is no general method to exclude negations of theorems; therefore, questions are not even effectively enumerable, so it might turn out that a well accepted answer is in fact a negation of a theorem. The paper does not contain any applications or examples.

Steinmann, M., Jr. (1959). "Questions and answers." *The graduate review of phil.* 1, 17–28. University of Minnesota, Minn.

Strawson, P. F. (1954). "A reply to Mr. Sellars." *Philosophical review* 63, 216–31.

This item is cited in the text, but it is not directly on questions.

Teller, P. (1974). "On why-questions." *Noûs* 8, 371–380.

Discusses certain difficulties of Bromberger 1966-b.

Tondl, L. (1969). "Logical-semantical analysis of the question and the problem of scientific explanation." *Proc. 14th International Congress of Phil. III,* Vienna, pp. 23–24.

—— (1970). "Semantics of the question in a problem-solving situation." *Problems of the science of science.* Special issue of the Polish quarterly *Zagadnienia naukoznawstwa,* pp. 79–101.

(Review by Zoltan Domotor: *JSL* 35, 1970, 314.)

—— (1973). *Scientific procedures.* Reidel, Dordrecht, Netherlands.

Chap. 5, sec. 1, is concerned with questions.

Waechter, W. (1967). "Problemstruktur und Problemverhalten in der wissenschaftlichen Forschung." *Deutsche Zeitschrift fuer Philosophie* 15, no. 1, 85–99.

Waismann, F. (1965). *The principles of linguistic philosophy.* Macmillan, London/Melbourne/Toronto. 422 pp.

The last chapter is "Towards a logic of questions."

Weinberger, O. (1970). *Rechtslogik.* Springer, Vienna and New York.

Chapter 12 is "Fragenlogik."

Whately, R. (1826). *Elements of logic*. 9th ed. John W. Parker, London, 1848,

Book 3, paragraph 9, is "Fallacy of interrogations." The other remarks on questions are quoted in Prior and Prior 1955.

Wheatley, J. (1955). "Deliberative questions."*Analysis* 15, 49–60.

"Deliberative questions" are questions calling for decisions, e.g. "What shall I draw?" "Shall I vote conservative at the next election?" According to Mayo 1956, it would be better to say that such questions call for an imperative as answer.

—— (1961). "Note on Professor Leonard's analysis of interrogatives, etc." *Phil. of science* 28, 52–54.

(Review by Gerold Stahl: *JSL* 31, 1966, 666–668.)

Wittgenstein, L. (1921). *Tractatus logico-philosiphicus*. Routledge and Kegan Paul, London, 1961.

Par. 4.0031: All philosophy is a "critique of language" (though not in Mauthner's sense). It was Russell who performed the service of showing that the apparent logical form of a proposition need not be its real one. Par. 6.5: When the answer cannot be put into words, neither can the question be put into words. The riddle does not exist. If a question can be framed at all, it is also possible to answer it. Par. 6.51: Scepticism is not irrefutable, but obviously nonsensical, when it tries to raise doubts where no questions can be asked. For doubt can exist only where a question exists, a question only where an answer exists, and an answer only where something can be said.

(For more detailed treatments of pseudoquestions see Carnap 1928, and Schlick 1935 and 1936.)

B. Linguistics

Arbini, R. (1969). "Tag-questions and tag-imperatives in English." *J. linguistics* 5, 205–214.
Bach, E. (1971). "Questions." *Linguistic inquiry* 2, 153–166.
Baker, C. L. (1968). *Indirect questions in English*. Ph.D. diss., University of Illinois, Urbana. University Microfilms, Ann Arbor, Mich., 1969.

—— (1970)."Notes on the description of English questions: The role of an abstract question morpheme." *Foundations of language* 6, 197–217.

Bakh, S. A. (1961). "K voprosu o strukture voprositel'nykh predlozhenij v sovremennom russkom jazyke (na materiale dram A. P. Chekhova)" (On a problem concerning the structure of interrogative sentences in the contemporary Russian language [using material from plays by Chekhov]). *Voprosy russkogo jazykoznanija*, pp. 95–108. Saratov, U.S.S.R.

Baligand, R., and James, E. (1973). "The intonation of wh-questions in Franco-Ontarian." *Canadian j. linguistics* 18, 89–101.

Behnstedt, P. (1973). *Viens-tu? Est-ce que tu viens? Tu viens? Formen und Strukturen des direkten Fragesatzes im Franzoesischen.* Tuebinger Beitraege zur Linguistik 41. Verlag Gunter Narr, Tuebingen. 325 pp.

> Contents: Die Frageformen in der "langue populaire"; Die Frageformen in der Sprache der Mittelschicht; Die Frageformen in der Rundfunksprache; Tabellen zur "langue populaire" und "langue familiére"; Umfragen zum Sprachgebrauch 1972; Soziolinguistische Analyse; Stilistische Analyse.

> (Review by J. Schmidt-Radefeldt: *Kritikon Litterarum* 3, 1974, 107–109.)

Berenshtejn, P. A., and Shramm, A. N. (1959). "O logicheskoj forme voprosa i grammaticheskikh sredstvakh ego vyrazhenija" (Concerning the logical form of the question, and the grammatical means of expressing it). *Uchenye zapiski Kaliningradskogo ped. instituta* vyp. 6, 189–227.

Berettini, P. (1969). "Richerche sulla frase interrogativa in greco antico." *Annali della Scuola Normale Superiore di Pisa: Lettere, storia e filosofia* 38, 39–97.

Bieringer, E. (1910). "Der mittel- und neufranzoesische Fragesatz." Diss. phil., Goettingen.

Bolinger, D. L. (1957). *Interrogative structures of American English (the direct question).* Publication of the American Dialect Society, no. 28. University of Alabama Press, University.

> (Review by R. B. Lees; *Word* 16, 119–125.)

(Review by P. Schachter: *International j. American linguistics* 25, 259-265.)

Borkin, A. (1971). "Polarity items in questions." In: *Papers from the seventh regional meeting of the Chicago Linguistic Society.*

Braun, F. (1966). "Die Ergaenzungsfrage als lexikalisches Phaenomen." Vortrag auf dem 1. Kolloquium ueber generative Grammatik in Hamburg. Mimeographed.

Braun, M. (1963). "Zur Intonation des Fragesatzes im Russischen." *Ivsicev zbornik,* pp. 15-23. Zagreb, Yugoslavia.

Bray, R. G. A. de (1968). "The pitch of Serbo-Croatian word accents in statements and questions." *The Slavonic review* 38, 380-393.

Bresnan, J. (1970). "On complementizers: Towards a syntactic theory of complement types." *Foundations of language* 6, 297-321.

—— (1972). "The theory of complementation in English syntax." Ph.D. diss., MIT.

Browne, E. W. (1972). "Conjoined question words and a limitation on English surface structures." *Linguistic inquiry* 3, 223-226.

Cattell, R. (1973). "Negative transportations and tag questions." *Language* 49, 612-639.

Chafe, W. L. (1968). "English questions." *Project on linguistic analysis reports,* 2d ser., no. 6, 1-60. Department of linguistics, Phonology laboratory, University of California at Berkeley.

—— (1970). *Meaning and the structure of language.* University of Chicago Press, Chicago.

There is a chapter on questions.

Chevalier, J. Cl. (1969). "Registres et niveaux de langue: Les problèmes posés par l'enseignement des structures interrogatives." *Le français dans le monde,* no. 69, 35-40.

Chistjakova, A. (1962). "O spetsifike voprositel'nogo predlozhenija." *Russkij jazyk v natsional'noj shkole,* no. 1, 12-18.

Conrad, R. (1968). "Ueber die Struktur russischer Fragesaetze." *Zeitschrift fuer Slawistik* 13, 201-208.

—— (1970). "Linguistische Probleme der Formalisierung von Frage und Antwort." *Linguistische Arbeitsberichte* 3, 22-30. Karl-Marx-Universitaet, Leipzig, E. Germany.

Crisari, M. (1975). "Sugli usi non instituzionali delle domande." *Lingua e stile* 10, 29-56.

(English and Russian summaries on p. 188 resp. p. 193.)

Danielsen, N. (1972). *Die Frage: Eine sprachwissenschaftliche Unter-suchung.* (Det konigelige danske videnskabernes selskab. Historisk-filosofiske skrifter 7, 1.) Munksgaard, Copenhagen.

Dubrawski, S. (1881). *Der slavische Interrogativsatz mit besonderer Beruecksichtigung der kleinrussischen Sprache.* Stry, U.S.S.R.

Egli, U. (1973). "Semantische Repraesentation der Frage." *Dialectica* 27, 363–370.

This is an introduction to the part on questions in Egli 1974. Com-pare the comments by Hintikka in his 1976-b.

—— (1974). *Ansaetze zur Integration der Semantik in die Grammatik.* Linguistik und Kommunikationswissenschaft 3. Scriptor, Kronberg, W. Germany. 139 pp.

In the part on questions (pp. 103–125) Egli proposes that they may be represented by lambda-expressions. "Who is coming" is rendered by "λx.x is coming." The idea is extended to the representation of questions in expressions of a λ-context-free-language. Such languages are extensions of Suppes-languages.

—— (1976). *Zur Semantik des Dialogs.* Sonderforschungsbereich 99 Linguistik, Universitaet Konstanz, Konstanz, W. Germany.

The methods of this paper are adapted from the works of R. Montague, Cresswell, D. Lewis; and Egli 1974. The paper contains an introduction and offers three theories of questions and answers: the first is an ex-plication of Carnap's operator "?"; the second is a development of the theory of questions in Egli 1974, whereas the third is an adaptation of Hamblin 1973. But instead of the Montague intensional logic, Tichý's intensional logic Lμ is used.

Fernandex, Ramirez, S. (1959). "La interrogacion." *Boletin de la Real Academia Española,* Madrid.

Flydal, L. (1965). "L'intonation interrogative et l'inversion, membres d'un paradigme heterogène?" *Proc. 5th International Congress of Phonetic Sciences,* Muenster, W. Germany, 1964, pp. 257–280. S. Karger, Basel, Switz. and New York.

Foulet, L. (1921). "Comment ont évolué les formes de l'interrogation?" *Romania* 47, 243–348.

—— (1926). "L'interrogation et l'ordre des mots en anglais et en français." *Romania* 52, 445–459.

Frei, H. (1968). "Réponse partielle et réponse totale." *Cahiers Ferdinand de Saussure* 24, 445–459.

—— (1970)."L'interrogation partielle et la distinction noyau-satellite." *Studies in general and Oriental linguistics, presented to Shiroo Hattori on the occasion of his sixtieth birthday,* pp. 103–108. Tokyo.

Freund, F. (1971). "Praepositionale und kasuelle Zeitangaben auf die Frage 'wann' im gegenwaertigen Deutsch." *Acta Universitatis Upsaliensis, Studia Germanistica* 8.

Friedmann, L. (1965). "Ueber die Modalitaet der deutschen Fragesaetze." *Zeitschrift fuer Phonetik* 18, 288–299.

Fromaigeat, E. (1938). "Les formes de l'interrogation en français moderne: Leur emploi, leurs significations et leur valeur stylistique." *Vox Romanica,* pp. 2–47.

Greive, A. (1974). *Neufranzoesische Formen der Satzfrage im Kontext.* Akademie der Wissenschaften und der Literatur, Mainz/Wiesbaden, W. Germany.

Grepl, M. (1965). "O vetach tazacich" (Interrogative sentences). *Nase Rec,* No. 5, 276–291.

Grundstrom, A. W., and Leon P. (1974). "L'intonation interrogative en français standard et en français canadien." *Studia phonetica* 9. Didier, Montreal/Paris/Brussels.

Haefele, J. (1974). "Fragekompetenz." *Germanistische Linguistik* 2, 171–205.

Harweg, R. (1974). "Retardierte Fragen." *Linguistics* 134, 9–20.

Hasegawa, K. (1970). "An aspect of English question formation." *Studies in general and Oriental linguistics, presented to Shiroo Hattori on the occasion of his sixtieth birthday,* pp. 198–206. Tokyo.

Helbig, G. (1974). "Was sind indirekte Fragesaetze?" *Deutsch als Fremdsprache* 11, 193–202.

Hermann, E. (1942). "Probleme der Frage." *Nachrichten der Akademie der Wissenschaften in Goettingen, Philologisch-Historische Klasse,* pp. 121–141.

—— (1943). "Herkunft unserer Fragewoerter." In: *Sitzungsberichte der Bayerischen Akademie der Wissenschaften phil.-hist. Abt.,* vol. 3.

Hirschbuehler, P. (1970). *Traitement transformationnel de l'interroga-*

tion et de quelques problèmes connexes en français. Diss., Université
Libre de Bruxelles, Belgium.
Huddleston, R. D. and Uren, O. (1969). "Declarative, interrogative and
imperative in French." *Lingua* 22, 1–26.
Hudson, R. A. (1975). "The meaning of questions." *Language* 51, 1–31.
Hundsnurscher, F. (1975). "Semantik der Fragen." *Germanistische
Linguistik* 3, 1–14.
Hull, R. D. (1972). "Towards a logical analysis of questions and an-
swers." M.A. thesis. Jesus College, Cambridge University. 61 pp.

Attempt to develop a "meaning representation" for questions.
Using a notation developed by Keenan for sentences, which-
questions are represented by means of a which-quantifier that gives
also the domain of the variable in question. For instance, "Who is
tired?" is represented by (wh man, x) (tired x) and "Who lives alone
and is tired?" by ((wh man, x) (lives alone x), y) (tired y). The
analysis is extended to yes/no-questions. Conditions for the truth of
an answer are given in the usual semantic terminology. Finally,
possible extensions of the notation to embedded questions, to
ambiguous questions, and to questions concerning the predicate are
discussed.

—— (1975). "A semantics for superficial and embedded questions in
natural language." In. E. Keenan (ed.), *Formal semantics of natural
language,* pp. 35–45. Cambridge University Press, Cambridge.
Hull, R. D., and Keenan, E. L. (1973). "The logical presuppositions of
questions and answers." In: D. Franck and J. Petoefi (eds.),
Praesuppositionen in Philosophie und Linguistik, pp. 441–466.
Athenaeum, Frankfurt.

A question-answer-pair (Q/A) is defined as follows: Q is a question
and A is a noun-phrase. (Q/A)-pairs are considered like propositions.
They have truth-values, and between them (and also other propositions) the relation of entailment is defined. Let S and T be
arbitrary sentences or (Q/A)-pairs; then, T is a presupposition of S
iff T is true in every state of affairs in which S is true or false (so S
is neither true nor false, but vacuous, whenever T is not true). Yes/
no-questions are represented by (Q/A)-pairs of the form $(S?/yes)$ or
$(S?/no)$. Finally some simple theorems on presupposition are proved.

Ibanez, R. (1973). "Programmatische Skizze: Intonation und Frage."
    In: H. J. Seiler (ed.), *Linguistic workshop 1*. Fink, Munich.
Imme, T. (1879, 1881). "Die Fragesaetze nach psychologischen
    gesichtspunkten eingeteilt und erlaeutert." *Programm des kaiser-
    lichen Gymnasiums zu Cleve.* Cleve, W. Germany.
Jespersen, O. (1924). *The philosophy of grammar.* Allen & Unwin,
    London.

   On questions, pp. 302–305.

—— (1940). *A modern English grammar on historical principles,* part 5.
    Allen & Unwin/Ejnar Munksgaard, London/Copenhagen 1965.

   On questions, pp. 480–512.

Kallioinen, V. (1965). "Les fonctions de l'intonation et la phrase inter-
    rogative en finnois." *Etudes Finno-ougriennes* 2, 107–122.
Karttunen, L. (forthcoming). "Syntax and semantics of questions."
    Linguistics and philosophy.
Katz, J. J. (1968) "The logic of questions." In: B. van Rootselar and
    J. F. Staal (eds.), *Logic, methodology and Philosophy of science
    III,* pp. 463–493. North-Holland, Amsterdam.

   (1) Short linguistic analysis of simple questions in terms of generative grammar. (2) Introduction of the notions "presupposition of a
   question," "possible answer," "refusal of a question," "evasion."
   A sentence *S* is an evasion to the question *Q,* iff *S* is a presupposition of *Q.* For example, *Q* can be: "what did John eat?" and *S*:
   "John ate something." *S* is a rejection of *Q,* iff *S* is inconsistent with
   the presuppositons of *Q.* For example, let *Q* be as before, *S* might
   be "John ate nothing." (3) Definition of "linguistically answerable
   questions" like "Who killed the man who was killed by John?" or
   "Where is the hat that is on my head?" (4) Finally the relation of
   entailment between questions is discussed and reduced to relations
   between answers.

—— (1972). *Semantic theory.* Harper & Row, New York.

   Chapter "Question," pp. 202–232.

Katz, J., and Postal, M. (1964). *An integrated theory of linguistic
    description.* MIT Press, Cambridge, Mass.

(Review by J. F. Staal: *Foundations of language* 1, 1965, 133-154.)

Kayne, R. S. (1973). "L'inversion du sujet en français dans les propositions interrogatives." *Le français moderne* 41, pp. 10-42 and 13-15.

Kholodilova, L. E. (1967). "Osobennosti znachenija voprositel'nykh predlozhenij s 'ne' pered skazuemym" (Semantic peculiarities of questions with negative predicates). *Russkij jazyk v shkole*, no. 2, 79-82.

Klammer, T. P. (1973). "Foundations for a theory of dialogue structure." *Poetics* 9, 27-64.

Klammer applies tagmemic theory as developed by Pike and others to dialogue structures. "Dialogue" is used in a rather comprehensive sense. In addition to sequences consisting of question and answer, other types of dialogue are investigated.

Kohler, K. (1973). "Phonetische und semantische Aspekte der 'tag questions' im Englischen." *Linguistische Berichte* 24, 35-42.

Konjukina, E. V. (1959). "Mestoimennye voprositel'nye predlozhenija, napravlennye na vyjasnenie obstojatel'stvennykh znachenij (po pamjatnikam XI-XVII vv.)." (Pronoun-questions; towards an understanding of adverbial significance). *Voprosy istorii russkogo jazyka*, pp. 250-275. Moscow.

Koutsoudas, A. (1968). "On wh-words in English." *J. Linguistics* 4, 267-273.

Kretschmer, P. (1938). "Der Ursprung des Fragetons und Fragesatzes." *Scritti in onore di Alfredo Trombetti*, pp. 27-50. Milan.

Krizkova, H. (1968). "Tazaci veta a nektere problemy tzv. aktualniho (kontextoveho) cleneni" (Interrogative sentences and some problems with them; actual [contextual] occurrences). *Nase rec*, no. 4, 200-210.

Kubarev, E. M. (1961). "Intonatsionno-otritsatel'nye predlozhenija v russkom jazyke v sopostavlenii s nemetskim i drugimi jazykami (s bolee podrobnoj kharakteristikoj odnoj iz takikh konstruktsij—predlozhenij s chastitsami 'razve', 'neuzheli')" (Negatively-intoned sentences in the Russian language, as contrasted with the German and kindged languages [with particular attention to one characteristic of such constructions—sentences with the particles "really" and "indeed"]). *Uchenye zapiski Kujbyshevskogo ped. instituta*, vyp. 31, 231-265.

Kuno, S., and Robinson, J. J. (1972). "Multiple wh-questions."
    Linguistic inquiry 3, 463–487.
Ladanyi, P. (1965). "Zur logischen Analyse der Fragesaetze (Abriss
    einer interrogativen Logik)." *Acta linguistica academiae scientiarum
    Hungaricae* 15, fasc. 1–2, 37–66.
Lafarge, A. (1974). "La phrase interrogative." In: *Documents et
    recherches-lettres,* no. 4, 3–4. Hâtier, Paris.
Lagane, R. (1965). "Eléments explétifs dans les phrases interrogatives
    et imperatives." *Le français dans le monde,* no. 35, 27–28.
Lakoff, R. (1973). "Questionable answers and answerable questions."
    In: Kachru, Lees, Malkiel, Pietrangeli, Saporta (eds.), *Issues in
    linguistics: Papers in honor of Henry and Renée Kahane,* pp. 453–
    467. University of Illinois Press, Urbana.
Lang, R. (1970). "Enga questions: structural and semantic studies."
    Ph.D. diss., Australian National University, Canberra.
Langacker, R. W. (1965). "French interrogatives: A transformational
    description." *Language* 41, 587–600.
—— (1970). "English question intonation." In: Sadock and Vanek
    (eds.), *Studies presented to Robert B. Lees by his students,* pp.
    139–161. Edmonton, Alberta, Canada.
—— (1972). "French interrogatives revisited." In: J. Casagrande and
    B. Saciuk (eds.), *Generative studies in romance languages,* pp. 36–69.
    Newbury House, Rowley, Mass.
—— (1974). "The question of *q.*" *Foundations of language* 11, 1–38.
Lawler, J. (1971). "Any questions?" In: *Papers from the seventh
    regional meeting of the Chicago Linguistic Society.*
Lehmann, Ch. (1973). "Wortstellung in Fragesaetzen." In: H. J. Seiler
    (ed.), *Linguistic workshop* 1, pp. 20–53. Fink, Munich.
Lojfman, N. Ja. (1957). "Perespros kak odna iz raznovidnostej
    voprositel'nykh predlozhenij v sovremennom russkom jazyke"
    (Cross-examination as one of a variety of interrogative sentences in
    contemporary Russian language). *Chkalovskij ped. instituta
    itogovaja nauchnaja konferentsija tezisy dokl.,* p. 31
—— (1958). "O nekotorykh voprosakh izuchenija voprositel'nykh
    predlozhenij" (On some problems in the study of interrogative
    sentences). *Uchenye zapiski Orenburgskogo ped. instituta,* vyp. 13,
    349–359.

Maas, U. (1972). "Ein Problem der Fragelogik: Sind zurueckgewiesene Praesuppositionen Antworten?" *Linguistische Berichte* 19, 69–73.

Malone, J. L. (1967). "A transformational reexamination of English questions." *Language* 43, 686–702.

Mal'tsev, M. D. (1949). "Zametki o voprosakh i voprositel'nykh predlozhenijakh prichiny i tseli v jazyke A. S. Pushinska" (Notes on questions about causes and reasons in the language of Pushkin). *Uchenye zapiski Leningradskogo ped. instituta* 76, 211–220.

Matveeva, M. L. (1957). "Funktsii voprositel'nykh slov v predlozhenijakh ritoricheskogo voprosa (na materiale publitsistiki A. I. Gertsena)" (The function of interrogative words in rhetorical questions [using material from the publications of Goertzen]). *Voprosy teorii i metodiki russkogo jazyka Chuvashskogo ped. instituta*, vyp. 2, pp. 244–265. Cheboksary, U.S.S.R.

Maury, N. (1973). "Observations sur les formes syntaxiques et melodiques de l'interrogation dite totale." *The French review* 47.

Meisel, J. M. (1974). "A possible constraint on wh-questions in French." In: Ch. Rohrer and N. Ruwet (eds.), *Actes du colloque franco-allemand de grammaire transformationelle*, vol. 1, pp. 122–138. Tuebingen.

Meunier, F. (1875). "Sur le passage du sens interrogatif au sens affirmatif." *Mémoires de la Societé Linguistique de Paris* 2, 246–260.

Mikhlina, M. L. (1957). "Javlenie nepolnoty v voproso-otvetnykh konstruktsijakh dialogicheskoj rechi" (The phenomenon of incompleteness in the question-answer structure of dialogue). *Uchenye zapiski (Dushanbinskogo) ped. instituta* 19, filosofskaja serija, vyp 9, pp. 85–122. Stalinabad.

Milner, J. (1973). "Analyse de la relation question-response en allemand." *Semiotica* 9, 219–240.

Moignet, G. (1966). "Esquisse d'une theorie psycho-mechanque de la phrase interrogative." *Langage*, no. 3.

Moravcsik, E. (1971). "Some cross-linguistic generalizations about yes-no questions and their answers." In: *Working papers on language universals.* Stanford University, Stanford, Calif.

Morin, Y. Ch. (1973). "Tag questions in French." *Linguistic inquiry* 4, 97–100.

Moroz, V. N. (1963). "O voprositel'nom predlozhenii" (On interrogative sentences). *Nauchnye trudy Tashkentskogo universita,* vyp. 211, fil. nauki, kniga 24, pp. 137–147.

Musić, A. (1908, 1910). "Pitanja u hrvatskom ili srpskom jeziku" (Interrogative sentences in the languages of the Croats and the Serbs). *Rad jugoslavenske akademije znanosti i umjetnosti,* knjiga 172, pp. 101–219; Zagreb, Yugoslavia, 1908. Knjiga 184, pp. 96–235; Zagreb 1910.

—— (1914). "Dodatak 'pitanjima u hrvatskom ili srpskom jeziku' " (More on interrogative sentences in the languages of the Croats and the Serbs). *Rad jugoslavenske akademije znanosti i umjetnosti,* knjiga 203, pp. 150–156.

—— (1934). "Interrogations dans la langue croate ou serbe." *Bulletin international de l'académie yougoslave des sciences et des beaux-arts,* book 1, fasc. 3, pp. 51–52. Zagreb, Yugoslavia.

Nehring, A. (1954). "Das Wesen der Fragesaetze." *Indogermanische Forschungen* 61, 40–54.

Nishnianidze, L. K. (1964). "Voprositel'nye predlozhenija v sovremennom russkom i grusinskom jazykakh" (Interrogative sentences in the contemporary Russian and Georgian languages). *Trudy Tbilisskogo universiteta,* vyp. 98, serija fil. nauk, pp. 197–216.

Noreen, A. (1901). "Tva olika slags fragesatser" (Two different kinds of question sentences). *Språk och stil* 1, 1–9.

Oomen, U. (1975). "Kommunikative Funktion und grammatische Strukturen englischer Fragesaetze." *Folia linguistica* 7, 43–59.

Osolovskaja, A. D. (1958). "Struktura prostogo voprositel'nogo predlozhenija s mestoimennymi slovami v sovremennom russkom jazyke" (The structure of simple questions with pronouns in the contemporary Russian language). *Uchenye zapiski Ul'janovskogo ped. instituta* 12, vyp. 2, 299–338.

—— (1959). "Voprositel'nye konstruktsii vnutri slozhnogo predlozhenija v sovremennom russkom jazyke" (Interrogative constructions within complex sentences in the contemporary Russian language). *Uchenye zapiski Ul'janovskogo ped. instituta* 15, vyp. 1, 33–52.

Patterson, G. (1972). "French interrogatives: a diachronic problem." In: J. Casagrande and B. Saciuk (eds.), *Generative studies in romance languages.* Newbury House, Rowley, Mass.

Paul, H. (1880). *Prinzipien der Sprachgeschichte.* 8th ed. Niemeyer, Tuebingen, 1968.

On questions, pp. 135-138.

Panfilov, V. M. (1963). "O mestoimennom voprose" (On pronominal questions). *Uchenye zapiski Krasnojarskogo ped. instituta* 25, vyp. 1, 83-89.

Peshovskij, A. M. (1956). "Vopros o 'voprosakh'" (A question about "questions"). In: A. M. Peshkovskij, *Izbrannye trudy,* pp. 33-49. Moscow.

Peterson, M. N. (1940). "O voprosakh" (Concerning questions). *Russkij jazyk v shkole,* no. 2, 38-40.

Pilipenko, O. F. (1962). "Intonatsija nemestoimennogo voprosa i svjazannogo s nim otveta v anglijskom jazyke (v sopostavlenii s ukrainskim jazykom)" (Intonation of the non-pronominal question and the connection with its answer, in the English language [in contrast with the Ukrainian language]). *Nauchnye zapiski Kievskogo ped. instituta inostrannykh jazykov* 5, 78-102.

Pinchon, J. (1967). "Les procédés interrogatifs." *Le français dans le monde,* no. 17, 47-49.

Pohl, J. (1965). "Observations sur les formes d'interrogation dans la langue parlée et dans la langue écrite non litteraire." In: G. Straka (ed.), *Actes et colloques du dixième congrès de linguistique et de philologie romane* 1962 vol. 2, pp. 501-513. Klincksieck, Paris, 1965.

Polikarow, A. (1966). *Elemente der Heuristik. Probleme des Aufbaus einer Problemtheorie.* Rostocker Philosophische Manuskripte, vol. 3. Rostock, E. Germany.

Pope, E. (1971). "Answers to yes-no questions." *Linguistic inquiry* 2, 69-82.

—— (1975). *Questions and answers in English.* Indiana University Linguistics Club, Bloomington.

In this study, Pope attempts to refine and extend the transformational analysis of questions in English presented in Katz and Postal (1964). Many of the revisions she suggests were motivated by a closer examination of the interaction between questions and their answers. In the case of rhetorical questions, she postulates a deep structure source different from that for non-rhetorical questions. This alternative source is designed to reflect the fact that rhetorical questions presuppose their answers. In the case of non-rhetorical questions (where she focuses mainly on yes-no questions), Pope shows that they do not presuppose, but rather are more or less strongly biased toward, one of their possible answers. She gives arguments, based on an analysis of rising and falling intonation, that yes-no questions are syntactically, as well as semantically, related to disjunctions. Finally, Pope shows that direct answers vary in acceptability, depending on the form of the question and the function of the answer.

Popov, A. (1879). "Orborot 'chto za . . . ' (was fuer ein) i srodnye s nim" (The expression "what sort of . . ." and related expressions). *Fil. zapiski,* vyp. 2, 1–12. Voronezh, U.S.S.R.

Pribylova, V. (1957). "K metodice tvoreni ruske otazky" (On the method of forming the Russian question). *Rusky jazyk* 7, no. 6, 264–269.

Py, B. (1971). *La interrogación en el español hablado de Madrid.* Brussels.

(Review by J. Schmidt-Radefeldt: *Kritikon litterarum* 3, 1974, 9–10.)

Raspopov, I. P. (1955-a). "O voprositel'nykh chastitsakh v sovremennom russkom jazyke" (On interrogative particles in the contemporary Russian language). *Trudy Blagoveshchenskogo ped. instituta* 6, 28–41.

—— (1955-b). "K voprosu o chastitsakh v sovremennom russkom jazyke (chastitsa 'li')" (On the question of particles in the contemporary Russian language [the particle "li"]). *Russkij jazyk v shkole,* no. 6, 17–19.

—— (1958). "Voprositel'nye predlozhenija" (Interrogative sentences). *Russkij jazyk v shkole,* no. 1, 34–37.

Regula, M. (1956). "Die Rolle der Frage im Sprachleben." *Zeitschrift Sprachforum* 1, 11–19, Muenster.

Renchon, H. (1967). *"Etudes de syntaxe descriptive, II: La syntaxe de l'interrogation.* Palais des Academies, Brussels.

(Review by P. Wunderli: *Vox Romanica* 30, 1971, 190–198.)

Restan, P. A. (1963). "Nabljudenija nad voprositel'nymi predlozhenijami v russkom literaturnom jazyke" (An observation on interrogative sentences in Russian literature). *Scando-Slavica* 9, 186–207.

—— (1966). "V'oprositel'noe predlozhenije, ego formy i funktsii (na materiale russkogo jazyka)" (The interrogative sentence, its form and function [using material in the Russian language]). *Scando-Slavica* 12, 132-148.

—— (1972). *Sintaksis voprositel'nogo predlozhenija* (The syntax of the interrogative sentence). Universitetsforlaget, Oslo. 880 pp.

Richters, O. (1910). *Zur historischen Syntax von interrogativem quel.* Diss. Phil., Goettingen.

Rodtwitt, E. (1953). *Ordstillingen i sporsmal hos Jean Anouilh* (Word order in questions in Jean Anouilh). Hovedoppgave, Universitet i Oslo, Norway.

Rohrer, C. (1971). "Zur Theorie der Fragesaetze" In: D. Wunderlich (ed.), *Probleme und Fortschritte der Transformationsgrammatik,* pp. 109-126. Hueber, Munich.

Romportl, M. (1955-1956). "Zum Problem der Fragemelodie." *Lingua* 5, 88-108

Ross, J. R. (1969). "Guess Who?" In: *Papers from the fifth regional meeting of the Chicago Linguistic Society.*

—— (1970-a). "Whether'-deletion." *Linguistic inquiry* 1, 146.

—— (1970-b). "Conjunctive and disjunctive questions." Presented at the first meeting of the New England Linguistic Society, Cambridge, Mass.

Sadock, J. M. (1970). "Whimperatives." In: Sadock and Vanek (eds.), *Studies presented to Robert B. Lees by his students,* pp. 223-238. Edmonton, Alberta, Canada.

—— (1971). "Queclaratives." *Papers from the seventh regional meeting of the Chicago Linguistic Society,* pp. 223-232.

—— (1974). *Toward a linguistic theory of speech acts.* Academic Press, New York.

Contents: Introduction; The evidence for the performative analysis; Embedded performatives; Indirect speech acts; Distinguishing use from meaning; Some covert illocutionary acts in English; Conclusions.

Sarles, H. B. (1970). "An examination of the question-response system in language." *Semiotica* 2, 79-101.

Schachter, Menzel, and Peterson (1968). "Interrogative." In: Stockwell, Schachter, and Partee (eds.), *Integration of transformational*

theories of English syntax, vol. 2, pp. 625–657. University of
California.

This is a preliminary, but unabridged, version of Stockwell, Schachter,
and Partee 1973.

Scherer, P. (1967). "The Gothic interrogative -u." *Proc. 10th International Congress of Linguists,* Bucharest, vol. 4, 461–464.

Schlyter, B. (1957) "Les types interrogatifs en français moderne."
Moderna språk 51, 99–115. Stockholm.

Schmidt-Radefeldt, J. (1973). "Zum metasprachlichen Fragesatz und
seiner Integration in die generative Semantik." *Linguistische
Berichte* 24, 43–53.

—— (forthcoming). *Aspekte einer Dialog-Theorie von Frage-Antwort-
Sequenzen (anhand des Deutschen, Franzoesischen und Portu-
giesischen).* Kiel, W. Germany.

Schreinecke, W. (1910). "Die Entwickelung des Modus im indirekten
Fragesatze des Franzoesischen." Diss. phil., Goettingen.

Shevela, J. (1956). *Skladba tazacich vet v evangelnich textech slovan-
skych* (Formation of interrogative sentences in old-church Slavonic
texts). Diplomni ukol, Brno, Czechoslovakia.

Shigarevskaja, N. A. (1963). "O strukture voprositel'nogo predlozhenija
v sovremennom frantsuzskom jazyke" (On the structure of the
interrogative sentence in the contemporary French language).
Vestnik Leningradskogo universiteta 2, 113–122.

Shil'derova, V. (1959). *Zamknutye voprosy v russkom jazyke* (Closed
questions in the Russian language). Diplomnaja rabota, Brno,
Czechoslovakia.

Shmelev, D. N. (1959). "O nekotorykh osobennostjakh upotreblenija
voprositel'nykh mestoimenij i narechij v razgovornoj rechi" (Some
peculiarities of usage of interrogative pronouns and adverbs in
ordinary language). *Russkij jazyk v natsional'noj shkole,* no. 66,
14–18.

Sivers, F. de (1965). "L'unité intonationnelle de l'interrogation en
hongrois." *Linguistique* 1, 75–112.

Smackey, T., and Beym, R. (1969). "Tag questions—dangerous psycho-
linguistic territory for TESOL." *International review of applied
linguistics* 7, 107–115.

Soell, L. (1971). "Der neufranzoesische direkte Fragesatz in einem Corpus der Kindersprache." In: *Sprache und Geschichte: Festschrift fuer Harri Meier,* pp. 493-506. Munich.

Staal, J. F. (1967). "Some semantic relations between sentoids." *Foundations of language* 3, 66-88.

(Review by G. H. Harman: *JSL* 35, 1970, 132-133.)

Sten, H. (1936). "Wiederholung des Verbums als Antwort." *Archiv fuer das Studium der Neuren Sprachen* 170, 229-234.

Stockwell, Schachter, and Partee (1973). *The major syntactic structures of English.* Holt, Rinehart and Winston, New York.

Chapter, "Interrogatives," pp. 600-632. Bibliography, p. 601.

Stourdzé, C. (1962). "L'inversion du sujet dans la phrase interrogative." *Le français dans le monde,* no. 12.

Sunden, K. F. (1919). "Betydelseskillnaden mellan fragesatsens bada huvudarter" (The difference in meaning between questions of the two main types). *Språk och stil* 10, 197-210.

Szmidt, Y. (1969). "Etude de la phrase interrogative en français canadien et en français standard." In: P. Leon (ed.), *Recherches sur la structure phonique du canadien français,* pp. 192-209. Didier, Paris.

Terry, R. M. (1966-67). "The frequency of use of the interrogative formula 'est-ce que'." *French review* 40, 814-816.

―― (1970). *Contemporary French interrogative structures.* Edition Cosmos, Quebec.

Turubull, P. (1963). "La frase interrogativa en la poesia contemporanea." *Boletin de la Real Academia Española,* pp. 473-605. Madrid.

Uldall, E. T. (1962). "Ambiguity: question or statement? or 'Are you asking me or telling me?'" *Proc. 4th International Congress of Phonetic Sciences,* pp. 779-783. Janua Linguarum, Series Maior 10. The Hague.

Ultan, R. (1969). "Some general characteristics of interrogative systems." *Working papers on language universals* 1, pp. 41-63a. Fink, Munich.

Urbancok, M. (1956). "Prispevok k triedeniu opytovacich viet" (A contribution to the classification of question sentences). *Jazykovedne studie* 1, pp. 213-227. Bratislava, Czechoslovakia.

Valimova, G. V. (1967). *Funktsional'nye tipy predlozhenij v sovremen-nom russkom jazyke* (Functional types of sentences in the contemporary Russian language). Izdanie Rostovskogo universiteta, U.S.S.R.

Valdman, A. (1967). "Norme pédagogique: Les structures interrogatives en français." *International review of applied linguistics* 5, 3–10.

Van Holk, A. G. F. (1975). "Semiotic aspects of the interrogative." In: W. Abraham (ed.), *Ut videam: Contributions to an understanding of linguistics. Festschrift fuer Pieter Verburg*, pp. 273–289. Peter de Ridder Press, Lisse, Netherlands.

Vannikov, Ju. V. (1957). "Klassifikatsija voprositel'nykh predlozhenij" (Classification of interrogative sentences). *Saratovskij ped. instituta, tezicy dokladov nauchnoj konf., posviashchennoj itogam nauchno-issledovatel'skoj raboty za 1956 god*, vyp. 4, 146–149.

Vodovozov, V. (1869). "O voprositel'nykh predlozhenijakh" (On interrogative sentences). *Uchitel'* 8, no. 15, pp. 482–485. Saint Petersburg.

Wachowicz, K. (1974). "Against the universality of a single wh-question movement." *Foundations of language* 11, 155–166.

Walther, J. (1976). "Zur Logik von Frage und Antwort." In: H. Weber and H. Weydt (eds.), *Akten des 10. linguistischen Kolloquiums Tuebingen 1975.*

Wandruszka, M. (1970). "Réflexions sur la polymorphie de l'interrogation française." *Revue de linguistique romane* 34, 65–77.

Weiser, A. (1975). "How not to answer a question: Purposive devices in conversational strategy." *Papers from the 11th regional meeting of the Chicago Linguistic Society*, pp. 649–660.

Wurm, A. (1953). "Odpovedi na dotazy" (Replies to questions). *Rusky jazyk* 3, 131–132.

Wunderlich, D. (1975). *Fragesaetze und Fragen.* Duesseldorf. Mimeographed.

Zacharias, C. (1966). "Die Intonation des Fragesatzes als Ausdruck seiner kommunikativen Funktion. Diss., Erfurt, E. Germany.

Zhinkin, N. I. (1955). "Vopros i voprositel'noe predlozhenie" (The question and the interrogative sentence). *Voprosy jazykoznanija*, no. 3, 22–34.

Zimmermann, G. (1970). "Aspekte der 'question disloquée'." *Die neueren Sprachen* 19, 486–491.

Zubaty, J. (1910). "Nali, nali-t'." *Listy filologicke* 37, 217–228.

The title is an old (16th century) Czech particle.

Zuber, R. (1972). "A propos de la question dite générale." *Dialectica* 26, 13–137.

C. Automatic Question-Answering

Barter, C. J. (1970). "Data structures and question answering." In: S. Kaneff (ed.), *Picture language machines,* pp. 341–374. Academic Press, London.

Bill, A. (1971). *A question-answering program for simple kernel sentences (QUE 2).* Microfiche. University of Texas, Austin.

Biss, K., Chien, R., and Stahl, F. (1971). "R2–a natural language question-answering system." *Proc. AFIPS Spring Joint Computer Conference,* vol. 38, 303–308. Atlantic City, New Jersey.

Black, F. (1968). "A deductive question-answering system." In: M. Minsky (ed.), *Semantic information processing,* pp. 354–402. MIT Press, Cambridge, Mass.

Bruce, B. C. (1972). "A model for temporal references and its application in a question answering program." *Artificial intelligence* 3, 1–26.

Chang, C., and Lee, R. C. (1973). *Symbolic logic and mechanical theorem proving.* Academic Press, London.

Contents: Introduction; The propositional logic; The first-order logic; Herbrand's theorem; The resolution principle; Semantic resolution and lock resolution; Linear resolution; The equality relation; Some proof procedures based on Herbrand's theorem; Program analysis; Deductive question-answering, problem solving, and program synthesis; Concluding remarks.

Dolotta, T. A. et al. (1976). *Data processing in 1980-1985.* Wiley-Interscience, New York.

This item is cited in the text, but it is not directly on questions.

Greene, C. C. (1969). *The application of theorem proving to question-answering systems.* Technical report no. CS138, Artificial Intelligence Group, Stanford Research Institute, June 1969.

Howe, W. G. (1969). "A logic of English questions with emphasis on automated query systems." Ph.D. diss. Northwestern University, Evanston, Ill.

Jardine, D. A. (ed.) (1974). *Data base management systems.* North-Holland, Amsterdam. 279 pp.

This item is cited in the text, but it not directly on questions.

Kraegeloh, K., and Lockemann, P. (1972). *Struktur eines Frage-Antwort-Systems auf mengentheoretischer Grundlage.* Berichte der Ges. fuer Mathematik und Datenverarbeitung no. 55. Bonn, W. Germany.

Kuhns, J. L. (1967). Answering questions by computer: A logical study. Memorandum RM-5428-PR. RAND Corporation, Santa Monica, Calif.

The main purpose of this work is to investigate the answering process. The formal representation of questions chosen is virtually that of Cohen 1929, namely to use free variables in place of wh-question words. The relation between formal questions and sets of values of the free variable of a given question formula is determined. A key problem is studied, namely the topic of "unreasonable" questions like "Who did not write 'Waverley'?" The concepts of definite, proper, and admissible formulas are offered as explications of the concept of reasonable questions.

—— (1969). *Logical aspects of question answering by computer.* P-4251. RAND Corporation, Santa Monica, Calif.

The paper contains an introduction and some addition to Kuhns 1967.

Martin, J. (1973). *Security, accuracy and privacy in computer systems.* Prentice-Hall, Englewood Cliffs.

This item is cited in the text, but it is not directly on questions.

Nevins, A. J. (1974). "A human oriented logic for automatic theorem-proving." *J. ACM* 21, 606–621.

A deductive system is described which combines aspects of resolution (e.g. unification and the use of Skolem functions) with that of natural deduction, and whose performance compares favorably with the best predicate calculus theorem provers.

Newell, A., Shaw, J. C., and Simon, H. A. (1960). "Report on a general problem-solving program." *Proc. International Conference on Information Processing* 1959, pp. 256–264. UNESCO, Paris.

This paper reports on a computer program, called "general problem solving program I" (GPS-1). Construction and investigation of this program is part of a research effort by the authors to understand the information processes that underlie human intellectual, adaptive, and creative abilities. The approach is synthetic—to construct computer programs that can solve problems requiring intelligence and adaptation, and to discover which varieties of these programs can be matched to data on human problem-solving. GPS-I grew out of an earlier program, "the logic theorist," and is an attempt to fit the recorded behavior of college students trying to discover proofs. The purpose of this paper is not to relate the program to human behavior but to describe its main characteristics and to assess its capacities as a problem-solving mechanism. The program should be seen as an attempt to advance our basic knowledge of intellectual activity and should not be assessed on whether it offers an economical solution to a significant class of problems. The major features of the program that are worthy of discussion are as follows: (1) the recursive nature of its problem-solving activity; (2) the separation of problem content from problem-solving technique as a way of increasing the generality of the program; (3) the two general problem-solving techniques that now constitute its repertoire—means-ends analysis, and planning; (4) the memory and program organization used to mechanize the program.

Nilsson, N. J. (1971). *Problem-solving methods in artificial intelligence.* McGraw-Hill, New York. 255 pp.

Contents: Introduction; State-space representations; State-space search methods; Problem-reduction representations; Problem-reduction search methods; Theorem-proving in the predicate calculus; Applications of the predicate calculus in problem solving; Predicate-calculus proof-finding methods.

Norton, L. M., and Slagle, J. R. (1973). "Experiments with an automatic theorem-prover having partial ordering inference rules." *Comm. ACM* 16, 682–688.

Overbeek, R. A. (1974). "A new class of automated theorem-proving algorithms." *J. ACM* 21, 191–200.

A procedure is defined for deriving from any statement S an infinite sequence of statements $S_0, S_1, S_2, S_3, \ldots$ such that: (a) if there exists an i such that S_i is unsatisfiable, then S is unsatisfiable; (b) if S is unsatisfiable, then there exists an i such that S_i is unsatisfiable; (c) for all i the Herbrand universe of S_i is finite; hence, for each i the satisfiability of S_i is decidable. The new algorithms are then based on the idea of generating successive S_i in the sequence and testing each S_i for satisfiability. Each element in the class of new algorithms is complete.

Palme, J. (1971). *Making computers understand natural language programming.* Edinburgh University Press, Edinburgh, Scotland.

Rosenbaum, P. A. (1967). "A grammar base question-answering procedure." *Comm. ACM* 10, 630–635.

The subject of this paper is a procedure for the automatic retrieval of certain segments of stored information, either explicitly or implicitly represented, through questions posed in natural language sentences. This procedure makes use of a sentence recognition device for the class of grammars, which will correctly decide between the grammatical and ungrammatical sentences of a natural language. It is possible to make use of a recognition device of this sort for the following reason: much data is fully expressible as a set of sentences in a natural language, a set which can be exhaustively and exclusively generated by a grammar. Based upon the rules of this grammar, a sentence recognizer will evaluate sentences, questions in the normal situation. Since the recognition function succeeds only when the posed question is drawn from the set of sentences expressing the data or, more correctly, is grammatical in terms of the grammar for this set of sentences, sentence recognition itself is a procedure for retrieving information. When the recognition function succeeds, its value represents the requested information.

Schank, R. C. (1971). "Finding the conceptual content and intention in an utterance in natural language conversation." *Proc. 2d International Joint Conference on Artificial Intelligence,* London, pp. 444–454.

The conceptual dependency analyzer described in the first IJCAI has been modified so as to function more conceptually with less reliance on syntactic rules. In order to have an analyzer be conceptually driven, it is necessary for the system to know what it is looking for. That is, it must make predictions as to what can follow conceptually at any point in the analysis. This paper discusses the extension of conceptual prediction to include predictions based on context and the structure of the memory model that operates with the analyzer. Such predictions make use of relations between conceptual actions and the implications of those actions. This enables the conceptual analyzer to discover not only the conceptual content of that utterance in context. We are concerned with the extraction of both the explicit and the implicit conceptual content in an utterance, in order to analyze effectively in an interactive conversational situation.

Schleichert, H. (1971). *Studien zur Interrogativlogik und automatischen Fragebeantwortung.* LB-Papier no. 16. Vieweg, Brunswick, W. Germany.

A FORTRAN program that does approximately the same job as the program of F. Black 1968.

—— (1972). *Studien zur Interrogativlogik und automatischen Fragebeantwortung: II. Das Programm BOOLETTE.* LB-Papier no. 27. Vieweg, Brunswick, W. Germany.

A FORTRAN program for deductive question-answering in the calculus of propositions.

Schwarcz, R., Burger, J., and Simmons, R. (1970). "A deductive question-answerer for natural language inference." *Comm. ACM* 13, 167–183.

Simmons, R. F. (1965). "Answering English questions by computer: A survey." *Comm. ACM* 8, 53–70. Also in: H. Borko (ed.), *Automated language processing,* pp. 253–289. John Wiley & Sons, New York, 1967.

—— (1970). "Natural language question-answering systems: 1969." *Comm. ACM* 13, 15–30.

Recent experiments in programming natural language question-
answering systems are reviewed to summarize the methods that
have been developed for syntactic, semantic, and logical analysis of
English strings. It is concluded that at least minimally effective
techniques have been devised for answering questions from natural
language subsets in small scale experimental systems, and that a
useful paradigm has evolved to guide research efforts in the field.
Current approaches to semantic analysis and logical inference are
seen to be effective beginnings but of questionable generality with
respect to either subtle aspects of meaning or applications over
large subsets of English. Generalizing from current small-scale
experiments to language processing systems based on dictionaries
with thousands of entries—with correspondingly large grammars and
semantic systems—may entail a new order of complexity and require
the invention and development of entirely different approaches to
semantic analysis and question answering.

Slagle, J. R. (1965). "Experiments with a deductive question-answering
program." *Comm. ACM* 8, 792–798.

(Review by D. C. Cooper: *JSL* 35, 1970, 596.)

Steel, T. B., Jr. (ed.) (1966). *Formal language description languages for
computer programming.* North-Holland, Amsterdam. 330 pp.

This item is cited in the text, but it is not directly on questions.

—— (1975). "Data base standardization—a status report." In: B. Dougue
and G. H. Nijssen (eds.), *Data base descriptions,* pp. 183–98. North-
Holland, Amsterdam.

This item is cited in the text, but it is not directly on questions.

Thompson, Lockemann, Dostert, and Deverill (1969). "REL: a rapidly
extensible language system." *Proc. 24th National ACM Conference,*
pp. 399–417.

Travis, L. , Kellog, C., and Klahr, P. (1973). *Inferential question
answering: Extending Converse.* System Development Corp., Santa
Monica, Calif.

The paper describes a deductive component developed for use by an
existing question-answering system. The emphasis is on deduction

within a question-answering context rather than within a mathematical inference system. The inference component was designed to find, for a given input question, the relevant general premises needed for deduction from a very large number of possible premises, most of which are irrelevant to any particular problem at hand. The inference system first constructs preliminary, skeletal derivation proposals. The purpose of these proposals is to find possible deductions before any attempt is made to verify the proposals. Verification is thus delayed until overall proof plans have been established. Later phases of processing examine the variable flow within a proposal to detect possible collisions and search the fact file for compatible sets of values for instantiation. The use of semantic information to aid deduction is incorporated into the system.

Westin, A. F., and Baker, M. A. (1972). *Data banks in a free society.* Quadrangle Books, New York. 522 pp.

This item is cited in the text, but it is not directly on questions.

Winograd, T. (1972). *Understanding natural language.* Academic Press, New York and London.

This paper describes a computer system for understanding English. The system answers questions, executes commands, and accepts information in an interactive English dialog. It is based on the belief that in modeling language understanding, we must deal in an integrated way with all of the aspects of language—syntax, semantics, and inference. The system contains a parser, a recognition grammar of English, programs for semantic analysis, and a general problem-solving system. We assume that a computer cannot deal reasonably with language unless it can understand the subject it is discussing. Therefore, the program is given a detailed model of a particular domain. In addition, the system has a simple model of its own mentality. It can remember and discuss its plans as well as carry them out. It enters into a dialogue with a person, responding to English sentences with actions and English replies, asking for clarification when its heuristic programs cannot understand a sentence through the use of syntactic, semantic, contextual, and physical knowledge. Knowledge in the system is represented in the form of procedural representations for syntax, semantics, and inference. We gain flexibility and power since each piece of knowledge can be a procedure; it can call directly on any other piece of knowledge in the system.

Woods, W. A. (1968). "Procedural semantics of a question-answering machine." *Proc. AFIPS Fall Joint Computer Conference,* vol. 33, 457–471.

D. Psychology and Pedagogy

Buelow, E. (1972). *Kommunikative Ethik.* Schwann, Duesseldorf. 303 pp.
Georgii, E. (1936). *Die Kunst des Fragens.* Verlag fuer Wirtschaft und Verkehr, Stuttgart. 47 pp.

Practical advice for the businessman concerning the art of putting the right questions in management and selling.

Harrah, D. (1973). "The logic of questions and its relevance to instructional science." *Instructional science* 1, 447–467.

This paper discusses the notion of a logic of questions, its relevance to instructional science, and the problems involved in developing a logic of questions that will be adequate from the standpoint of instructional science. Several systems of question logic—particularly those of Belnap and Åqvist—are noted. The notion of a pedagogical question, in a wide sense of "pedagogical," is discussed. A system adequate to deal with pedagogical questions will be an erotetic logic in a wide sense of "erotetic," covering not only individual interrogative sentences but also sets of sentences of various kinds, and sets of appropriate replies of various kinds. An erotetic logic of this sort is outlined in the paper and more fully in the appendix. Questions are then raised concerning its adequacy.

Kreibig, J. H. (1914). "Beitraege zur Psychologie und Logik der Frage." *Archiv fuer die gesamte Psychologie* 33, 152–212.
Loew, F. (1928). "Logik der Frage." *Archiv fuer die gesamte Psychologie* 66, 357–436.

Contents: Das Wesen der Frage; Der Fragesatz als Ausdruck; Die Deutung der Frage als seelisches Geschehen; Zur Struktur des

Wissens; Das Wissen als Wunschziel; Die notwendigen und hinreich-
enden Bestandteile der Frage; Frage und Antwort; Sur Einteilung der
Frage; Ueber das Verhaeltnis der Fragen zueinander; Ueber die
Beantwortbarkeit der Fragen; Die Frage in der geistig-seelischen
Realitaet.

Meux, M. O., and Othanel Smith, B. (1970). *A study of the logic of
teaching*. University of Illinois Press, Urbana. 231 pp.

Kochan, B., and Kochan, D. (1971). "Problemloesung durch Frage-
strategien: Eine Lerneiheit zur Sprachfoerderung im 5. Schuljahr."
Die Deutsche Schule 63, 246–258.

Martinak, E. (1906). "Das Wesen der Frage." *Atti del V. congresso
internazionale di psicologia,* Rome, pp. 333–336.

Pawlowski, T. (1969). "Theory of questions and its applications to
social sciences." *Polish sociological bulletin* 20, 95–109.

Petzelt, A. (1962). *Von der Frage. Eine Untersuchung zum Begriff der
Bildung*. Lambertus, Freiburg i. Br., W. Germany. 190 pp.

Robinson, W. P., and Rackstraw, S. J. (1972). *A question of answers*
(2 vols.). Routledge and Kegan Paul, London. German edition:
Soziolinguistische Untersuchungen ueber Antworten. Schwann,
Duesseldorf, 1973.

Contents: Outline of research; The question-answer exchange;
Aspects of answers—the analysis system in application; Restricted
and elaborated codes and answering; Answers of five-year-old
children to "wh"-questions; Answers of mothers to children's
questions; Answers to "wh"-questions; Seven-year-old children;
Answers to "wh"-questions in relation to Bernstein's theory; appendix A—Sample transcripts of mothers' and children's answers;
Content validity of the taxonomic scheme; Content validity of the
taxonomic scheme—empirical data; The taxonomic scheme—summary
and conclusions; Appendix B—Coding frame for answers to "wh"-
questions; Appendix C—The questions asked of seven-year-old
children.

Smith, N. C. (1974). "A question-answering system for elementary
mathematics." Ph.D. diss., Stanford University.

Tumlirz, O. (1919). *Das Wesen der Frage: Beitraege zu ihrer Psychologie, Gegenstandstheorie und Paedagogik*. Leipzig. 160 pp.

Contents: (I) Beitraege zur Psychologie und Gegenstandstheorie der Frage: Der problematische Charakter der Frage; Objekt, Objektiv, Dignitativ und Desiderativ; Die psychologischen Voraussetzungen der emotionalen Erlebnisse; Die psychologischen Voraussetzungen der Frage; Der unbestimmte angeeignete Gegenstand und das Interrogativ; Akt und Inhalt des Fragebegehrens; Das Wesen der Antwort; Die Arten der Frage; Zusammenfassung. (II) Beitraege zur Paedagogik der Frage: Der Streit zwischen alter und neuer Paedagogik—Lehrerfrage, Schuelerfrage; Der psychologische Charakter der Scheinfragen; Der psychologische Charakter der Schuelerfrage; Die geistigen Entwicklungsstufen der Jugendlichen—(a) die Entwicklungsstufen, (b) die Interessen; Innerhalb welcher Grenzen interessieren sich die Jugendlichen fuer die Bildungsstoffe der Schule; Sollen die Bildungsziele der Schule den natuerlichen Interessen der Jugend geopfert werden?; Das Anwendungsgebiet der Lehrerfrage; Die Moeglichkeiten der Schuelerfrage; Zusammenfassung.

Wunderlich, D. (1969). "Unterrichten als Dialog." *Sprache im technischen Zeitalter* 32, 263–287.

Index

To avoid needless repetition, we assume an automatic cross-reference from "interrogative" to "questions"—we have usually used the latter in this index even where the former occurs in the text.

We have not indexed notation separately. If you know what the topic is but not what the henscratches look like, consult this index under the entry "notation for." On the other hand, if you have got some puzzling henscratches, a look through the List of Numbered Displays, beginning on p. 149, should eventually send you to the right place.

A subentry such as *1965* under "Åqvist" refers to the corresponding item in the bibliography. If such a subentry bears a page number less than 139, consult part A of the bibliography; otherwise, part C. Since initials are given there, we include full names here only for individuals not listed in the bibliography, or to disambiguate.

We prepared this index with the assistance of Bindex, a system of computer programs designed to lessen some part of the agony of indexing. For information, consult the University of Pittsburgh Computer Center, or NDB.

vs. hypothetical questions, 95, 101
of yes-no type, 103–04
conditioned interrogatives, 103
conditions, 8, 19
of conditioned interrogatives, 103,
105
range of, 9
conjuction, 7
infinite, 107
many-place, 7
of questions, 89–90
of relativized interrogatives, 105–06
conjunctive questions
and decomposition of questions, 90
direct answers to, defined, 89
and partitions of questions, 138
consistency, 10, 122
containment of questions, 136
Harrah-, 137
corrections-accumulation question sequences, 91
corrective answers, 15, 47, 129
just-, 129
and nominal/real distinction, 129
standard, 129
Corr(I), 130
criteria, 68–69. *See also* erotetic logic,
criteria for

data-base management systems, 139,
142
erotetic logic and, 145
improvability of, 144–45
recent research on, 144
use in inquiry systems, 142–44
data-processing industry
and computer sciences, 141
growth of, 140, 142
problems in software, 141
theoretical base of, 140–43
decomposition of questions, 90, 138
denotation, 9
description-questions, 79–82
descriptors, 79
desiderata, 78

determinables, 80
determining, 29
d(I), 108
direct answers, 12–13
abstract, 71
contrasted with other replies, 13–16
and corrective answers, 15
in deep structure, 15
effectivity of, 3
form of, and questions, 34
fundamentality of, 3, 35
and intentions of questioners, 13
parts of, 34, 68
and presuppositions of questions,
113, 124
to a question or interrogative,
defined. *See under each type of
question or interrogative; also* notation for
real, 72
relative to models, 102, 103
disjunction, 7
of questions, 89
distinctness-claims, 34, 60–67
in answers to elementary questions,
68
examples of, 66
in a modal language, 61*n*
need for, 60–61
and nominal/real distinction, 61–62
notation for, 64
in query systems, 67
for unionized subjects, 93
distinctness-claim specifications
of description-questions, 81
empty, 61
lexical, 65
need for, 61–63
no intermediate ones, 61
nonempty, 61
notation for, 65
in requests of elementary questions,
68
for whether-questions, 64
Dist(σ,S), 64–65